Nature's Grace

American Liberal Religious Thought

Don Crosby and W. Creighton Peden
General Editors

Vol. 2

PETER LANG
New York • Washington, D.C./Baltimore • San Francisco
Bern • Frankfurt am Main • Berlin • Vienna • Paris

Marvin C. Shaw

Nature's Grace

Essays on
H. N. Wieman's Finite Theism

PETER LANG
New York • Washington, D.C./Baltimore • San Francisco
Bern • Frankfurt am Main • Berlin • Vienna • Paris

Library of Congress Cataloging-in-Publication Data

Shaw, Marvin C.
  Nature's grace: essays on H. N. Wieman's finite theism / Marvin C.
Shaw.
    p. cm. — (American liberal religious thought; vol. 2)
  Includes bibliographical references (p.   ).
  1. Wieman, Henry Nelson, 1884–1975. 2. Theism— History of
doctrines—20th century. I. Title. II. Series.
BX4827.W45S48   230'.092—dc20   94-33887
  ISBN 0-8204-2707-1
  ISSN 1080-5389

Die Deutsche Bibliothek-CIP-Einheitsaufnahme

Shaw, Marvin C.:
Nature's grace: essays on H. N. Wieman's finite theism / Marvin C.
Shaw. - New York; Washington, D.C./Baltimore; San Francisco; Bern;
Frankfurt am Main; Berlin; Vienna; Paris: Lang.
  (American liberal religious thought; Vol. 2)
    ISBN 0-8204-2707-1
NE: GT

Cover design by George Lallas.

The paper in this book meets the guidelines for permanence and durability
of the Committee on Production Guidelines for Book Longevity of the
Council on Library Resources.

© 1995 Peter Lang Publishing, Inc., New York

Printed in the United States of America.

Contents

Foreword

Between 1926 and 1968, Henry Nelson Wieman produced a number of books that established him as the premiere empirical theologian of the time. Along with Douglas Clyde Macintosh, he made constructive use of empirical methods, leading, in Wieman's case, to a naturalistic theism. His continuing significance is evident in this book by Marvin Shaw.

Wieman was continuously in conversation with other theologians. In 1932, he joined Macintosh and Max Otto in a three-way conversation that continued for twenty-five weeks in the *Christian Century*, later published in the book, *Is There a God?* Robert L. Calhoun of Yale and Wieman discussed theology in a series of articles in *Christendom* in 1936–1937. He and John Dewey argued about Dewey's book *A Common Faith* in *Christian Century* in 1934. He worked with others in several books: Regina Westcott Wieman, Walter Marshall Horton, and Bernard Eugene Meland. He responded to eighteen critics and commentators in *The Empirical Theology of Henry Nelson Wieman* (edited by Robert W. Bretall) in 1963. When Macintosh suggested that I write my dissertation on Wieman and others of the Chicago School in 1935, I found the basis for my own empirical theology.

It is clear that many people of various religious outlooks have been affected by the boldness of Wieman's approach. Those who have known him have been impressed by him as a person. For him religion was, like baseball, a passion. Students have said that one should examine Wieman's face when he was leading a group in prayer.

Wieman's development was consistent. He began by stressing the significance of religious experience, analyzing it with rare critical insight. His brilliant interpretation of mysticism in *Religious Experience and Scientific Method* (1926) was reiterated in *Man's Ultimate Commitment* (1958), and as late as 1971 he still retained this position, although he had been understating it because of possible misinterpretation.

Wieman thought of himself as a philosopher of religion. Theologians are limited by their traditional vocabulary and loyalty to a particular tradition within a specific religion, where philosophy of religion seeks to analyze experience beyond any limitations. He suggested that the philosopher of religion is like a dietitian who knows what the food consists of and the theologian is like the cook who provides a tasty meal. But if we start with Wieman's early position, as suggested by Bernard Meland, we can gain a perspective that will help us with the rest of Wieman's writings. Wieman tended to disregard these early insights, and even suggested that people interested in his thought should start by reading *The Source of Human Good* (1946), but, as we have seen , he never lost his base in a kind of mysticism. However, he did discard his interpretation of Whitehead's metaphysics and concept of God after his initial warm treatment of Whitehead in *The Wrestle of Religion with Truth* (1927).

Marvin Shaw has undertaken an important task in providing an up-to-date interpretation of Wieman's thought. In the early 'seventies he wondered if he was the only person interested in Wieman until he met Larry Axel of Purdue. He discovered that empirical theology is alive and influencing other theological positions. His associates in the Highlands Institute for American Religious Thought have produced a volume on empirical theology. (See *Empirical Theology: a Handbook* edited by Randolph C. Miller, Birmingham, Alabama, Religious Education Press, 1992.)

Wieman persisted during the World War II years when neo-orthodoxy dominated the American scene. He and Bernard Meland were lone voices for empirical theology. But while the "death of God" controversy scuttled much of neo-orthodoxy, Wieman said that its leaders were not talking about his God, for his concept met the empirical demand for verification. Both Wieman and Meland continued to publish for another decade or longer. When I published my *The American Spirit in Theology* in 1974, I dedicated it to Wieman.

Shaw describes naturalistic theism in its development in the Chicago School, including Edward Scribner Ames and Shailer Mathews, who were already established scholars before Wieman arrived. Wieman wanted to increase the specificity of the concept of God arising from this naturalistic empiricism.

In chapter two, Shaw deals with what he calls the middle period of Wieman's developing thought. This was when he saw God as a creative synthesis at work throughout the universe. It is worthy of supreme loyalty and devotion because it is the religious support for human life. It is what Shaw calls "nature's grace." It is fully natural, and yet superhuman. Emerging good may replace existing goods, causing disruption and suffering, and to deal with this, human nature needs to be open to constant transformation. How one adjusts to this reality for which all concepts are unreliable and conducive to idolatry, Wieman spells out in his *Methods of Private Religious Living* (1929). Human beings cannot succeed alone in reaching a transformed state but must rely on nature's grace.

Shaw then moves back to the earlier books in which Wieman established his empirical methodology and provided a concept of God which is empirically grounded. He not only established the *how* but the *what*. In his interpretation of religious experience, he made use of Whitehead's principle of concretion, which provides order in the cosmos as well as wholeness in human beings. But Wieman could not remain satisfied with this formulation and moved on to seeking God empirically in human relationships.

The Source of Human Good shows more influence from Dewey than from Whitehead. It is focused on what transforms human beings. Yet this is more than humanism, for human beings cannot accomplish this transformation by themselves; they must rely on a process that transcends them but remains within the natural world. This creative good is good under all conditions. Thus there is a basis for value that calls all human values into question and opens the quest for further and higher values. This creative event is not all-powerful.

Shaw also discusses Wieman's relations with John Dewey and William Bernhardt, and concludes with chapters on mysticism and Christology.

I believe that Wieman was a Christian mystic who was hardheaded and honest enough to discard most traditional theological concepts while he sought to keep the central insights in terms that match the thinking of the modern world. He became a Unitarian without denying his Presbyterian background, which was more honest than many who are closet Unitarians within traditional churches.

Marvin Shaw is to be congratulated on presenting to modern readers an interpretation of Wieman's thought and nature's grace that will help us to understand not only Wieman but ourselves.

Randolph Crump Miller
Horace Bushnell Professor of Christian Nurture Emeritus
Yale Divinity School

Acknowledgments

Nature's grace is tangible and ever-present. Gratitude is expressed to Professor Cyril K. Gloyn, onetime professor of philosophy at Occidental College, for introducing me to the thought of Henry Nelson Wieman (who taught at Occidental from 1917 to 1927); the late Daniel Day Williams, Roosevelt Professor of Systematic Theology at Union Theological Seminary, a patient and supportive teacher; my associates in the Highlands Institute for American Religious Thought, and especially Cedric Heppler and Professors W. Creighton Peden, Nancy Frankenberry, Charley Hardwick, and Jerome A. Stone; the late Professor Larry E. Axel, who helped me overcome the illusion that I was the only person still interested in Wieman by introducing me to a circle of Wieman scholars at a meeting of the American Academy of Religion in 1974; Professor Donald A. Crosby for his energetic and perceptive editorial assistance; and my wife Jeanne Paul Shaw for her love, help, and patience.

Nature's grace is manifest in second chances. Earlier versions of some of these chapters appeared in professional journals; every such chapter has been completely re-written, supplemental materials have been added in every case, and in most instances the original thesis has been revised. Permission to use previously published materials has been granted by the journals. Parts of the first, second, and seventh chapters appeared in *Encounter* (Christian Theological Seminary); a quite different version of chapter three was published by *Journal of Religion* (University of Chicago Press); *Zygon: Journal of Religion and Science* (Chicago Center for Religion and Science) printed an earlier version of chapter four; one section of chapter six served as a chapter in *Creative Interchange: Essays in Honor of Henry Nelson Wieman* edited by J.A. Broyer and W.S. Minor and published by Southern Illinois University Press.

Introduction

The sun was about the breadth of a hand above the low cliffs that formed the west bank of the Missouri, and as I looked down the grassy slope of the Park College campus toward the road and over the buildings beyond it the thought came to me that I was seeing something like what the young Wieman saw from his dormitory window in 1907. I stopped walking toward the chapel and dropped out of the gaggle of professors and let them pass me by; they continued to talk and gesture not noticing my absence. Shading my eyes against the glare of the late sun, I could see that near the opposite shore there was a long, thin sand bar with some struggling scrub-growth on it. I decided that Wieman could not have seen just this strip of mud and vegetation since the river constantly shifts and changes, and many spits of mud had come and gone in seventy-five years.

It was four months before his twenty-third birthday, and he was in his senior year at Park College intent on becoming a journalist, when a scene like the one before me provoked in him a decisive experience. Years after the event he described it in these words.

> I came to my room after the evening meal and sat alone looking at the sunset over the Missouri River. Suddenly it came over me that I should devote my life to the problems of religious inquiry. I never had a more ecstatic experience. I could not sleep all night and walked in that ecstasy for several days. Since that evening in April I have never doubted my vocation.[1]

This is a puzzling statement and the description is clearly shaped by later decisions and clarifications in a long career as philosopher-theologian. Wieman said that at the time of the experience he probably would not have described it as centering on intellectual inquiry, and so we may wonder if it was actually a moment of religious insight.[2] I think not, because he says that the result of this experience was not a decision to become a clergyman like his father, and he relates it rather to the influence of a course in comparative religion taught by Joseph McAfee and to that of others he had taken in philosophy with Silas Evans.

Wieman was raised in a household pervaded by a warm and traditional but undogmatic sense of God's reality and presence. While he could not remember any doctrinal statement in his father's sermons, he recalls the sense of the reality of family prayer at meal-time. He once said that throughout his life he never doubted the reality of God.[3] As you read on this claim may seem enigmatic, since in the following chapters you will see that the philosopher Wieman did not believe in a personal, supernatural God. I believe that through his early studies at Park he came to see the great variety of beliefs about the divine reality, and the philosophical naivete of many of them; yet he continued to experience the reality of grace. He seemed to be asking, if the traditional beliefs about the divine are false, then what is it that in fact works in human life with the sustaining and saving power we experience? Years later he described the problem that motivated all of his work as the desire to answer this question.

> What operates in human life with such character and power that it will transform us as we cannot transform ourselves, saving us from evil and leading us to the best that human life can ever reach, provided we meet the required conditions?[4]

Through his study of comparative religion and philosophy the young Wieman seems to have come to doubt traditional beliefs about God, and yet he was convinced that religious practices place people in relation to an actual, transforming power. If we see the contradictions between the various accounts of God and yet continue to encounter supportive currents and fulfilling forces in our lives like those faithful people have always known, we must seek to discover their actual source. If for philosophical reasons we no longer believe in the reality of a realm beyond natural, observable events, then religious commitment and self-giving must center on a yet-to-be-discovered aspect of the world of events rather than on the myth of the transcendent King or Father. And so Wieman devoted himself to the quest for a concept of the divine creative activity as an observable aspect of the world of natural events.

∗ ∗ ∗ ∗ ∗

Henry Nelson Wieman's father was undertaking his first pastoral charge as a Presbyterian minister in Richhill, Missouri, when the young Wieman was born August 19, 1884. Henry was the first-born of eight children. The family lived in Richhill, and then in the towns of Irving and Corning in Kansas. In Wieman's ninth year, the family moved to the lower San Joaquin Valley in California. He attended two years of high school there, and then took the final two years of preparatory study at the academy attached to Occidental College, a Presbyterian school in Los Angeles. He said that during this time he read John Fiske's *Destiny of Man* (1884) and concluded, with his father's agreement, that Christianity and evolution are entirely compatible. The freshman year at Occidental was academically unsuccessful because of Wieman's involvement in football and student government, and he transferred to Park College in Missouri. Park was also a Presbyterian-related school but very different from Occidental; students were obligated to earn part of their tuition and expenses by working on the college farm and in the construction of its buildings. Wieman's mother graduated from Park and taught there three years, and the family hoped that the discipline of the work-study college would benefit Henry. Here he met Anna Orr, who was to be his wife. Wieman received the bachelor's degree from Park in 1907.

Wieman insisted that even after the experience described above he had no interest in becoming a minister of religion; however, a theological seminary represented the only opportunity for the advanced study of religion. His first choice was the liberal Union Theological Seminary, which prided itself on being a "graduate school of religion" independent of denominational control, but because of his mother's illness and the desire to be near his family he attended a rather traditional Presbyterian institution, San Francisco Theological Seminary in San Anselmo, California. Wieman found the study of biblical criticism and church history irrelevant to his own quest; he did not want to understand the history of traditional beliefs about religious reality but to discover its actual nature and operation. The core of the theological curriculum was Calvinism, as interpreted by the nineteenth-century divine Charles Hodge. Wieman regarded Calvinism as somewhat ridiculous, but in order to compete for the seminary's traveling fellowship he studied Hodge and Calvin's *Institutes*, although he claims it was like learning a foreign language. He did later admit, however, that the fundamental Calvinist belief in the need for transforming grace which works beyond human effort remained with him all his life.

Wieman received the bachelor of divinity degree in 1910, when he was twenty-six, and his success in winning the traveling prize took him to Europe in the fall of that year. He studied with the philosopher Rudolf Eucken at Jena, and at Heidelberg with the historian of philosophy Wilhelm Windelband and the liberal theologian Ernst Troeltsch. Wieman's single-minded interest in his own inquiry as he understood it, and his feeling that tradition in philosophy and theology were of little relevance to this interest, led him to say later that these two years were disappointing and contributed little to his development.

In 1912 he returned to Missouri, married Anna Orr, and was ordained as a Presbyterian minister; he served for about two and a half years in St. Joseph, Missouri, and Davis, California, devoting more time to the reading of Henri Bergson than to sermon preparation. The great French Jewish philosopher of evolution taught Wieman to see reality as a creative process in which new forms emerge, rather than as the mechanistic interaction of changeless entities. Wieman was anxious to pursue his religious inquiry, and leaving his wife and children with relatives in Missouri, he commenced to study for the doctoral degree in the department of philosophy at Harvard University. His choice was largely influenced by the desire to work with William Ernest Hocking, author of *The Meaning of God in Human Experience* (1912); in Hocking he hoped to find a way of identifying the divine creative activity as observably operative in the events of life. He says that he sincerely attempted also to absorb and affirm Hocking's idealist metaphysics, but he could not. Wieman received the Harvard doctorate in philosophy in 1917.

From 1917 to 1927 he taught philosophy at Occidental College. While in Los Angeles, Wieman read the first philosophical works of the mathematical physicist Alfred North Whitehead, *The Concept of Nature* (1920) and *Science and the Modern World* (1925). In Whitehead's metaphysical analysis, Wieman found the process view of reality present in Bergson without Bergson's anti-intellectualist substitution of intuition for reason. Wieman published his first book, *Religious Experience and Scientific Method*, in 1926, and the first chapter of this book appeared as an essay in *Journal of Religion*.[5] The philosopher John Dewey made approving comments on the article, and this brought Wieman to the attention of the many Deweyans at the University of Chicago. Edward Scribner Ames invited Wieman to teach during the summer session at Chicago, and while a visiting instructor at McCormick Theological Seminary the following autumn term, Wieman presented a talk on Whitehead's latest book, *Religion in the Making* (1926). Shailer Mathews, then dean of the Divinity School of the University of Chicago, offered Wieman a permanent position. As we will see in the first chapter, Ames and Mathews hoped that Wieman would be able to combat the growing influence of the religious humanism of A. Eustace Hayden and others.

Wieman's most important work was done between 1927 and 1947, while he taught at Chicago. In 1932, Anna died of cancer. Wieman's second wife, Regina Westcott, was a psychologist and cooperated with him in writing a book on the psychology of religion.

As we will see, Wieman shifted from an interest in the speculative metaphysical vision of Whitehead toward more empirical and observational thinking; and he shifted from an interest in the divine as a creativity active throughout the evolving universe to a narrow focus on creativity in human psychology. As time passed, he also became less confident that he would find a hearing for his naturalistic and empirical ways of thinking about God within traditional religious denominations. At Chicago Wieman had known both members of the Federated Theological Faculty and students who were associated with Meadville Theological Seminary, a Unitarian school. After his retirement from Chicago in 1947, he taught briefly at the University of Oregon in Eugene, and at the invitation of a former Chicago student who was a Unitarian clergyman, he became a member of the Unitarian church. In 1950, without demitting the Presbyterian ministry, he received fellowship as a Unitarian minister. Wieman taught as a visiting professor at Washington University in St. Louis and at Grinnell College in Iowa, and then from 1956 to 1966 undertook a second career in the department of philosophy of Southern Illinois University in Carbondale. During this period, his work was most closely focused on the way creativity works in human communication. After his second retirement, he served as visiting professor at two Unitarian institutions, Starr King School for the Ministry in Berkeley and Meadville in Chicago.

For years Wieman participated in the conferences of the Institute for Religion in an Age of Science at the Isle of Shoals off the coast of Maine, and through this association he participated in the founding of the journal *Zygon: Journal of Religion and Science.*

After an illness of a year and a half, Wieman died of Parkinson's disease June 19, 1975 in Grinnell, Iowa, while in the care of his third wife, Laura. He was to have received the Unitarian-Universalist Association's Award for Distinguished Service to the Cause of Liberal Religion, and the honor was bestowed posthumously at a meeting of the General Assembly of that denomination later in the month of his death.

* * * * *

Wieman saw his life work as the attempt to understand that saving, transforming power encountered in religious living as an observable process at work in the natural world; he never doubted its presence and reality but thought that traditional myths and symbols give no knowledge of its character. Perhaps the technical details of his thought about the divine creative activity can best be understood if we look at a second decisive experience in his personal life.

Wieman first reported this event in *Religious Experience and Scientific Method* in 1926, without indicating that it was his own experience; in a later essay he stated that it was a report of an occasion in his own life which occurred in 1916, while he was a doctoral candidate at Harvard.[6]

> I had been separated from my wife and children for over a year. I felt under compulsion to continue my studies but must also support my family, and, if possible, have them with me instead of remaining where they were, halfway across the continent. I could do this only if I could get a certain kind of work that could be carried along with my studies. I made several attempts to get such work but failed. Finally, I received a tentative offer, providing I could make good. The first time I came I was very nervous, being worn with much study and having lived in much isolation in the attempt to complete the work for my degree. I did not do myself justice. I came a second time and at the close of the day was told that my employers were not satisfied with my services and that I could not have

the position. It was nine o'clock at night at the time. I had to ride many hours on the interurban to reach my place of residence. I shall never forget that long ride of misery. It was after two o'clock a.m. when I got to bed. I could not sleep although I was worn with nervous strain, the day's work, and disappointment.

The hours of the night were almost unendurable. Worse than the disappointment and failure to find a means of seeing my family was the sense of my own worthlessness and futility. I felt completely beaten. It was total loss of self-confidence. It was not this last failure alone that overthrew me, but a series of experiences during the two previous years, which I had interpreted as failures. Because of these experiences I had been fighting the sense of failure and futility for some time. Now it rose up and crushed me quite completely. I had no inclination to suicide (although the thought occurred to me), because it appeared to be about the meanest thing I could do toward those who were dependent upon me. But it occurred to me that if I had only myself to consider I should certainly have gladly welcomed any means of ending the misery and futility of it all.

During the forenoon of the next day I attended to certain duties and in the afternoon returned to my room to face the facts as squarely and completely as possible and somehow find myself. I felt there was something [that] must be fought out and settled, although I could not tell just exactly what it was. I suppose it was a vague sense that I must settle the problem of living my life and my relation to things in general. I felt there could be no rest for me until I settled things somehow.

I spent about four hours in my room alone. It was not exactly thinking, nor exactly praying, although at times it was one or another of these quite distinctly. Most of the time, I suppose, it was a sort of combination of these. Gradually there emerged within me a spreading sense of peace and rest. That almost unendurable pain of mind that had possessed me for twenty-four hours assuaged and passed away quite completely. I imagine it passed somewhat as a pain passes under an anesthetic. Then I found myself filled with a strange new exuberance. I was almost laughing and crying with joy. Joy about what? I could not tell. I only knew my pain was gone, and I was full of great gladness, courage, and peace. All the facts were exactly as they had been and I saw them more plainly than ever. My family was still as far away as ever and there was no visible means of getting them any closer. My failure to get the work I wanted stood as it had before. I cannot say that I had any anticipation of how my difficulties might be overcome. I did not even have the feeling that they would be overcome. I simply knew that I was glad, and ready and fit to go ahead and do whatever I might find to do and take the consequences whatever they might be. There was no hysteria and no hallucination about it. The strong emotion of gladness gradually passed away in the course of days, but the courage, peace, readiness to meet any fortune with equanimity, and joy in living did not go away. The old anguish did not return.

> In the course of time I was able to have my family with me, but we spent
> the winter fighting to save the life of our youngest. For six weeks his life
> hung in the balance and for many days we had to watch over him con-
> stantly day and night. At one time he lay apparently dead and was only
> restored by artificial respiration. Yet through all this the old feeling of
> dejection and failure never recurred. Instead, a deep inner feeling of calm
> and divine presence was with me. In the years since then I have not kept
> to this high level, but I feel I have discovered the sources of infallible
> support in any time of need.[7]

While I do not mean to suggest that this experience is the primary
source of Wieman's way of thinking of the divine creative activity,
we do see within his recollection of it certain themes essential to his
thought. In a little known essay on mysticism and religious experience written more than forty years after the occurrence, Wieman
says that he does not really understand the event nor trust any of
the traditional interpretations which might be given, but he nevertheless attempts an interpretation of his own.

Wieman distinguishes this type of religious experience from those
which purport to be disclosures of divine beings or truths about
them. He sees his experience as of a second type in which painful
and even unendurable perceptions come to be integrated into a new
and broader experience which is itself satisfying. Wieman sees his
crisis as typical of those provoked by what the existentialist Karl
Jaspers calls "ultimate situations" such as death, guilt, misfortune,
loss, failure, suffering, and rejection; these moments may cause the
breakdown of those protective devices which shield us from dis-
turbance. Then we either develop new defenses and deceptions, or
we undergo a sort of rebirth. In the latter case, the mind is reorga-
nized so that experience is deeply satisfying, although it includes
elements which by themselves caused anxiety and despair. A level
of consciousness is reached which recognizes the dark realities of
failure, rejection, and guilt and still affirms the goodness of life. The
question for Wieman is how this comes about.

The key for Wieman is that this state of mind cannot be reached
until the reality and magnitude of ultimate situations is recognized
and the defensive narrowing and numbing of consciousness to avoid
perceiving them is abandoned. We then see that those aspects of our
present lives which we prize, and the increase of this sort of good
that we desperately hope for in the future, are both in fact perish-

able and precarious, and we let go of both the achieved and the hoped for goods. When we are liberated from clinging to these specific goods, we may become aware of that creativity which gave rise to them and which will build new orders when they are gone. Here the threatened or lost values are relativized by being brought into relation with the vision of the larger self which may emerge through that grace which Wieman calls creativity.

> When all envisaged goods actual and possible seem as nothing compared to what the total self demands and seeks, and the apparent limitation of human existence seems unendurable, then the self can be liberated from preoccupation with achieved goods, subject as they are to destruction and impoverishment. When the self is thus liberated and in this condition seeks with uttermost self-giving to find what can make life livable, creativity can rise to dominance over anxiety and despair and all other concerns.[8]

This sort of religious experience involves letting go of attachment to created good and opening oneself to the as yet unknown possibilities implied in creativity. The root idea here is the distinction between that which is created and that which creates, a distinction fundamental to all theistic belief. We are free from the fear of loss when we withdraw our commitment from the created and give ourselves over to creative transformation. The fundamental character of this insight will become apparent in the discussion of Wieman's rejection of pantheistic resignation, in Chapter Five.

Wieman contrasts this mysticism of rebirth with the mysticism of revelation. In the transformative type of experience, we undergo radical change in the way we perceive, interpret, and evaluate our experience. The religious significance of this experience is not that it points beyond the world of natural events to a transcendent realm, but that it manifests a creativity operating in the human mind and in interpersonal relations.

Recall Wieman's insistence that the resolution of his problem did not involve any actual change in the arrangement of his life: he still had no job, was separated from his family, and had the same past history of what seemed like failure. What he received was a new way of seeing things. And this event confirmed to him that there is a creativity at work in the mind that transforms us in ways we could not anticipate, so that we experience the world with greater awareness of its richness and plasticity. At his best, Wieman says that this progressive integration of the mind is a manifestation of a process of progressive integration at work beyond and before human life on all levels of the evolving universe; it is one form of a creativity pervading all existence.

*   *   *   *   *

The following chapters represent a study of Wieman's attempt to develop a specific concept of this creativity manifest in the natural world; in this attempt he sought a concept of the divine creative activity as an observable process at work in natural events. In the first chapter we will encounter the so-called naturalistic theism of Edward Scribner Ames, Shailer Mathews, and Wieman. We will notice the difference between the generalized conception of nature's creative supportiveness of human life in Ames and Mathews and Wieman's more focused attempt to develop a description of a particular structured event which manifests creativity in nature and human life. The second chapter will examine Wieman's work of the 'thirties in which this type of recurrent event is described as progressive integration or creative synthesis; the thesis of this study is that Wieman's enduring contribution is found here. The next chapter is a study of Wieman's concepts of the divine before and after this period. It presents Wieman's earlier attempt to make use of Whitehead's concept of the principle of concretion in an attempt to understand creativity, and his effort to relate this speculative construct to a phenomenology of religious experience. Wieman's growing commitment to a Deweyan empiricism led him to set aside this passing interest in Whiteheadian metaphysics. The same chapter shows the full extension of this empiricism, as Wieman turned away from the idea of creativity as a tendency observed throughout inorganic and organic evolution and became increasingly focused on creativity in the mind and communication.

Wieman's naturalistic theism differs from two other definitions of the religious ultimate available within naturalism: pantheism and humanism. Thus, the next two chapters center on the analysis of two debates in which Wieman participated, one centered on Dewey's humanism and the other on the pantheism of Wieman's student, William Bernhardt. Additional chapters focus on Wieman's life-long interest in the study of mysticism and religious experience, and on his interpretation of the historical Jesus.

Years of teaching Wieman to undergraduates lead me to make the following warnings regarding the interpretation of the words "grace" and "creativity." As used in Wieman's writings, creativity does not mean a human power manifest in artistic or scientific work, the application of talent and effort. It is a technical term used to refer to all those instances in both the human and non-human worlds in which relations of mutual support and enhancement are woven, and novel integrations achieved. Creativity discloses nature's fundamental character and is thus prior to human aptitude and action. Similarly, as I use the term in interpreting Wieman, grace does not mean human gracefulness or graciousness, the human quality of grace under pressure, or any other human trait. I use the term as it is generally used in Christian theology to indicate an unmerited gift, help beyond our own contrivance or merit from a source not ourselves.

Chapter One

Naturalistic Theism

To understand the somewhat odd and intriguing creation of religious reflection called naturalistic theism, we must return to a debate conducted within the faculty of the Divinity School of the University of Chicago during the third and fourth decades of this century. A number of the participants in this discussion had accepted a naturalistic view of the world, and it seemed that humanism was the only option left for religious thought. If the supernatural, second-story of the universe is denied, then it seemed to many that the object of religious commitment ought to be the increase of human welfare; humanism must replace theism, they maintained. In this controversy a unique approach to the concept of the divine was developed as an alternative to religious humanism. So our first project is to understand the character of the naturalistic theism of the Chicago Naturalists, and to distinguish it from supernatural theism, pantheism, and panentheism.

Views of the Divine within Naturalism

There seem to be four logically possible approaches to the question of the relation of nature and the divine: exclusion, identity, and the two forms of inclusion. God and nature might exclude each other because they exist in different ways, one being the supernatural creator and the other created. Or, nature and the divine may be identical, two names for the same reality, two ways of seeing one great fact. Or, one might include the other: the natural world might be a part of a divine life that transcends it, or, as strange as it sounds at first, nature might include the divine as one factor or tendency.

If you think of these four possible relations as a continuum, then you can imagine two additional types of interpretation of the terms as forming the two extreme poles; these extremes would not be

interpretations of the relation of nature and the divine, but the assertion of one term, together with the denial of the other. God alone
might be real and nature a mere appearance, or the natural world
might be all there is while God is the illusion.

Thus we have a continuum of six possible types of interpretations
of nature and the divine: exclusion, identity, the two forms of inclusion, and the two ways in which one term is accepted and the other
rejected. If D is the divine and N nature, we have:

1. D   2. D/N   3. D(N)   4. D=N   5. N(D)   6. N

(1) *Theistic monism* is the belief that the divine alone is real, and
that nature is at best a mere appearance. Perhaps this is the view of
that aspect of Vedantist thought called "unqualified non-dualism" and
associated with Sankara. (2) *Theistic dualism* is the assertion that the
divine is wholly transcendent over nature, a totally different kind of
reality which could only be known if it disclosed itself in a revela-
tory act in the world. This may be seen in the classical theism emphasized in the Western tradition. (3) *Panentheism* claims that the divine
transcends but also includes nature. Charles Hartshorne's form of
process philosophy represents this view. In each of these first three
ways of relating nature and deity, the divine is in some sense transcendent over the everyday world, whereas this is not the case in
the next three.

(4) *Pantheism* believes that the divine and nature are in some sense
identical. This is intended in the sense that nature is itself divine,
and so it is not the same as theistic monism, and is exemplified in
Greek Stoicism or the philosophy of Spinoza. (5) *Immanent Theism*
asserts that nature includes the divine; thus the divine is not transcendent over nature in any sense. Many forms of polytheism are of
this type, insofar as the gods are seen as subject to the exigencies of
fate and the conditions of nature; but other forms of polytheism portray the gods as transcendent over nature, and these might be
instances of theistic dualism. Various forms of naturalistic and
evolutionary theism developed in the late nineteenth and early twen-
tieth centuries are of this type, and one of these is the subject of this
book. (6) *Atheism* is the belief that nature alone is real, and that the
divine is either an illusion or an imaginal representation of aspects
of the natural world. One form of atheistic belief proposes an object

of religious devotion different from God or the gods. Religious humanists assert that the focus of religion should be the ideal of human fulfillment, and our attempts to reconstruct nature and society so as to embody this ideal. We will see later that this is the approach of John Dewey.

The naturalists we will be dealing with take nature as the all-inclusive category. Everything that happens has a cause, and nature is the order of causes; every existent is an event or some aspect of events, and everything we have to deal with in life is within this order of events. Then it follows that the first three types of belief are rejected by naturalists because they all involve some notion of the divine transcendence over nature.

The three views of the object of religious devotion logically possible for naturalists would therefore seem to be (a) that nature as a whole or in some fundamental aspect has the value of the divine; (b) that the religious ultimate is human good, the ideal vision of human fulfillment which guides reconstructive effort; or (c) that the divine consists of those aspects of nature upon which human fulfillment depends. We will be referring to these views as pantheism, religious humanism, and naturalistic theism. Each takes the object of religious commitment as natural rather than as transcendent over nature.

George Santayana (1863–1952) seems to have set the pattern that dominated naturalistic discussions of religion in America, when he insisted that the divine must be interpreted from the point of view of human good. Nature taken as a whole both sustains and destroys human ends, and has no special regard for human life. Thus, to worship nature is to accept whatever nature does; it is to abandon human interests as the standard of value. According to Santayana, in pantheism we worship not goodness but power.

Santayana's critique of pantheism can be stated more fully. The stance toward the world that is natural to humanity is one in which events are evaluated as to whether they sustain or obstruct human interests. Human ideals arise as the imaginative vision of the fulfillment of human interests, and they are, according to him, our natural object of devotion. But plainly, nature both fulfills and frustrates human interests. Therefore, the worship of nature as a whole requires an artificial and forced abandonment of our natural and unavoidable commitment to human good. In pantheism, we abandon the perspective given in our own being, and identify instead with nature, substituting for our commitment to the fulfillment of human life a self-denying resignation which accepts whatever nature happens to bestow. Santayana found this outlook in Greek Stoicism and in the idealism of his teacher Josiah Royce. He believed that while a balanced view of life recognizes the appropriateness of acceptance and resignation when we are confronted with that which cannot be changed, to adopt this attitude to life as a whole and in advance is to set aside our natural love of human good and the hope that it may increase.[1]

As a matter of historical fact, the American naturalists did not at first endorse pantheism, although we will later study a well-known debate between Wieman and his former student William Bernhardt on this issue, and more recently, others associated with Chicago Naturalism have come to a pantheistic position.[2] But the discussion among religious naturalists was initially between humanists and naturalistic theists. And in this discussion the influence of John Dewey (1859–1952) was pervasive.

Dewey agreed with Santayana that religious life centers on the ideal of a fulfilled human life. But Dewey had a thoroughly "contextualist" view of the ideal; the ideal is not a human imposition on natural events but arises in the context of the interaction of human and non-human. It is not an idle and wishful dream, but a vision of ways in which natural conditions and human interests may be harmonized. Ideal visions arise when natural conditions are seen from the point of view of human needs and interests; they are suggested by natural conditions, as a possible perfecting of nature's tendencies which our efforts may bring about. That human good to which Dewey as a religious humanist is devoted is itself created and sustained in the interaction of humans and natural conditions. Notice that this idea involves a view of nature as supporting intelligent effort, and not as simply indifferent or hostile.

This notion of our ideal visions as themselves rooted in nature's powers and tendencies suggested to some naturalists an approach to religion different from Dewey's. For him, in the process in which the ideal is generated and comes to be embodied, the creative element is human vision and effort. But should not human effort itself be viewed contextually, as taking place within and dependent upon its natural context? Naturalistic theism is the result of a modification of Dewey's analysis of the interaction of human and non-human;

in this approach, what is actually creative of the good is the inter-action as a whole rather than the human factor primarily. In such a view, the divine is the more than human, but wholly natural, source of good. In a later chapter concerning a notable exchange between Wieman and Dewey, we will see how Dewey's humanism is subject to this re-interpretation.

What is at stake in the debate between humanists and naturalistic theists is ultimately practical and personal rather than theoretical and abstract. In one view, the creative factor in the process through which human good grows is human intelligence and effort. In the other view, emphasis is placed on the creativity of the non-human context of life. Thus, in humanism a self-understanding centered on activity and control is encouraged, whereas in naturalistic theism, we are to cultivate openness to superhuman sources of transforma-tion. The difference is that between the attitude of self-reliance and the awareness that our efforts are dependent upon factors which underlie them and to which we must in some sense submit. In nat-uralistic theism, as will be seen, we seem to have the theistic stance without the supernatural god.

Now it is possible to present a definition of naturalistic theism. In this view, the divine is those aspects of nature upon which the good of human life depends; here, the divine is superhuman but natural, functionally transcendent of human effort, but not ontologically tran-scendent of the natural world. This view is naturalistic because the divine is conceived as within and not beyond the natural order; and it is theistic because the divine is not merely the ideal vision of human good and our efforts to embody it, but the larger natural context upon which both the conception and realization of the ideal depend.

The Chicago Naturalists

Interesting forms of naturalistic theism were developed in the midst of the conflict of theism and humanism within the Chicago faculty. For some, the implications of the naturalistic world-view clearly demanded a humanistic interpretation of religion. Naturalistic the-ism arose within this controversy as an attempt to move beyond humanism, while accepting its naturalistic assumptions. Thus, nat-uralistic theism appears as a mediating position between classical theism and religious humanism.[3]

This mediating role is seen in the changes of opinion which the discussion engendered. The humanistic view was represented by A.E. Haydon, and seems at first to have been shared by E.S. Ames.[4] Ames' early position seems to have identified the divine with the spirit of the social group, following the anthropologist Emile Durkheim. In Ames' book *Religion* (1929), this concept provides the starting point of his discussion, but it is broadened to include nature as generating and supporting group values. A complementary shift in position resulting from participation in the discussion of theism and humanism is seen in Shailer Mathews. In his *Faith of Modernism* (1924) his views are a form of immanent, personalistic theism related to nineteenth century idealistic thought, while in *The Growth of the Idea of God* (1931) his position is clearly a naturalistic theism. Thus, naturalistic theism is a result of the convergence of humanism and traditional forms of theism.

Edward Scribner Ames: the Divine as Idealized Reality

In common with other American naturalists, Ames felt that the time had come to set aside the dualism of humanity and nature which has characterized modern thought since Descartes. He used a contextualist theory of value like that of Dewey to show that values are not subjective impositions on a dead and valueless mechanical world, but are disclosures of the qualities resident in nature which arise in interaction with goal-seeking organisms. Values can be taken as clues to the character of the natural interactions which produce them.[5] As we will see, the concept of the divine is an attempt to formulate the value of nature in relation to human life and refers to actual characteristics and functions of nature.

To Ames, the non-dualistic view of reality developed in American naturalism makes it possible to shift from the view of mind as a separate substance beside the body and the world of objects to a view of the mind as the body's intelligent behavior. Similarly, the divine need no longer be sought as a separate object. For just as value is the way objects function in human experience, so the divine is the way nature as a whole functions in experience.[6]

In Ames' view the divine is an observable behavior of the world; it is ". . . the reality of the world in certain aspects and functions— in what is here characterized as reality idealized."[7] The divine is the interpretation of reality from the point of view of human values. The naturalism of Ames overcomes the dualism of ideal and natural, so that the divine may be characterized either as the ideal, considered as including those aspects of nature upon which it depends, or as nature, considered as supportive of the ideal.

These alternative expressions will form the basis of the exposition of Ames' view of the divine. In discussing the first, the divine as the human good and its basis in nature, Ames seems to argue against humanism; and in discussing the second, nature insofar as it supports human good, he seems to be a critic of pantheism.

Religion is seen by Ames as based upon devotion to the values of the group. "Religion . . . is the cherishing of values felt to be most vital to our life and blessedness, by means of ceremonial dramatization, expressive symbols, and doctrinal beliefs."[8] Hence, in its historical forms the concept of the divine reflects and embodies the values arising from the life- experience of a people. In this sense, the divine represents the spirit of a people.

> . . . [J]udgments of morals and truth constitute a frame of reference through which all reality is measured. By that frame the conception of God is assessed. Some things are not worthy to be attributed to God any more than to a noble person. And certain characteristics are inevitably identified with reality, conceived as God. At any stage of culture, what is good in humans is good in their God, and while . . . the progressive changes in the idea of God . . . [correspond] to different levels of morality, it is apparent that the character of God reflects the best as people feel it for themselves.[9]

The ideals of the group do not, by themselves, simply constitute the concept of the divine; rather, the divine is the outcome of the interpretation of nature from the point of view of a group's values.[10]

As such, the divine is not merely figmental or imaginary; it is a certain organization of natural factors and energies, human and non-human. The divine is constituted from the point of view of the ideal, but the ideal must be understood as including its natural conditions. The divine has the substance of the actual world of things and people.

> God is the spirit of the world of living beings, taken in their associated and ideal experience. God includes the so-called material world which is the stage of their action and the condition of their existence, and God signifies also the order of their intelligence and conduct. God is the grand total,

living process, in which they live and move and have their being. . . . God
is their world, idealized and personified in accordance with their deepest,
most spiritual insight and endeavor.[11]

In defining the divine from the point of view of human values, Ames
avoids the simple identification of the divine with the ideal considered apart from the natural processes which it expresses. The identification of the divine with the human ideal was current in much of
the humanism of the time in which Ames wrote, and he felt that this
view reflected the dualism of humanity and nature.

> The idea of God may thus be seen to express more than the mere projec-
> tion of human ideals, for that expression still carries within it the old dual-
> ism between an alien cosmos and our little world of interests and values.
> No doubt the ideals arise in human experience, but they are not on that
> account to be discredited by saying that they are merely human. They are
> as real as the body or the rock on which the body rests, and they are as
> much a part of the cosmos.[12]

The divine is the ideal considered as the outcome of a tendency of
nature.[13]

Conversely, the divine may be defined as nature, insofar as it
sustains the ideal. Ames points out that his view differs from pantheism just as it differed from humanistic devotion to the ideal above.
The divine does not include all of nature, but that which fosters the
good. "God is not equivalent to all reality but to certain phases of
it."[14] Thus the divine is reality as "ideally evaluated;"[15] that is, the
concept of the divine selects those aspects of nature upon which
human good is thought to depend.

> God is reality idealized. This idealization does not mean fabricated or imag-
> ined. It means selection. God is the world of life taken in certain of its aspects,
> in those aspects which are consonant with order, beauty, expansion.[16]

In the notion of the divine as reality idealized, the term "idealized"
connotes selection or evaluation on the basis of relevance to human
values; it does not mean simply perfected in the imagination. Ames
notes three aspects or functions of nature as supportive of human
good and as therefore included in the divine: orderliness, love, and
intelligence. Each is considered as present in nature, though not
prevalent, and together they constitute the matrix in which human
life is nurtured. The divine is thus reality understood as manifesting order, love, and intelligence, and as thereby fostering human

good. In this way, the divine is identified with actual and observable aspects of experience.

It might seem to the reader that nature does not in fact manifest intelligence as distinct from order, and that it does not manifest love; rather, these appear to be human traits. But recall that the approach of the American naturalists is based on the claim that nature is not to be understood, as in mechanistic materialism, merely as a system of dead matter and blind force; nature is only seen truly when we include within it human life and nature's potential for sustaining it.

As reality contains much that runs counter to these three aspects selected by the term *God*, the question arises as to why human good is utilized as the selective criterion at all. Ames' answer is that most concepts, including that of the divine, are developed as tools employed in the attempt to achieve a fuller life, and that they are justified through their usefulness in that process. However pessimistic religions have been, and however much they have included the tragic dimension in their symbols, the divine has always been identified "with the will to attain the good through the dominance of order, intelligence, and love."[17] Nevertheless, a realistic estimate of human experience reveals that the processes in nature upon which the good of human life depends are not entirely dominant over counter-processes; thus the concept of the divine as idealized reality must be considered a finite God.[18]

In Ames' way of speaking, the divine is a term of selection, a concept denoting assorted aspects of nature valued as functioning in a certain way. Yet it is no more "empty" than any other concept, since all ideas are developed as selections of aspects of experience for attention. The only test of this or any other concept is whether it makes a relevant and useful discrimination of factors encountered in experience. In addition, Ames seems to maintain that the factors selected by the term *God* do not constitute a miscellaneous collection, but an active order.

> God as Reality, inclusive and ideally evaluated, is not to be thought of apart from that Reality. It is no more strange that religion should have this general term than that science should have the word "Nature," or that politics should speak of "World," or that philosophy should conceive the "Cosmos." If these are "concrete universals" may not God also be a concrete universal? Any universal is used to gather up facts and experiences into a system, to designate the system in which they are known to stand.

It is therefore more than a class term, indicating a number of particulars. Such a universal means an organization of factors into a whole. Thus "city" signifies more than "people," for a city presents associations of people in certain relations, geographical, political, and economic. The term God expresses order and purpose and moral values in the great Reality which we call Life or the World. Reality conceived as friendly, as furnishing support for human existence and for the realization of ideal ends, is God.[19]

Apparently Ames concludes that the divine as reality idealized is not a congeries of factors incidentally supportive of the good in various discrete situations, but certain constant features ingredient in every instance of the growth of good. This is suggested in his choice of order, love, and intelligence as the major aspects of nature selected by the term God. That is, the divine is not a mere collection of items relevant to human goals; rather, use of the term denotes that the world is so constituted that goods are generated and sustained. It is not that we envision a goal and then seek for those miscellaneous natural energies providing the leverage necessary to its achievement; instead, human life as embedded in nature reveals in the very fact of its existence a certain constant character or order generating human life and possibilities of good, and supporting efforts to achieve them. This seems to be the intent of Ames' distinction between a mere term of selection and a concrete universal.

Evidently, Ames would feel that there is an important aspect of reality which we would overlook if we did not have the concept of God. For Ames the meaning of the divine as a term in the interpretation of nature is that in important respects human life takes place in a friendly environment; we are at home in the universe. A person's devotion to God

carries . . . the conviction that God is on the side of our deepest sense of right and good. Or at least we believe that the world, when taken in all its aspects, includes a moral order or is capable of supporting such an order. . . . The religious attitude is therefore one of confidence toward reality and experience, with reference to the values which we at our best cherish most profoundly. This is a quality of disciplined optimism.[20]

Human effort, therefore, has meaning and a reasonable hope of success, especially if it takes account of the necessities present in natural conditions. Seen in the light of the divine, our effort takes on the added dignity of being a needed contribution to the gradual growth of good.

Shailer Mathews: the Divine
as the Personality-Producing Activities

Naturalism in American philosophy results from the attempt to inter-pret human life as included within nature. The result is that human life and culture are naturalized and nature is in some sense human-ized; that is, humanity is seen as a manifestation of powers and poten-tials latent in nature, and nature is understood as capable of producing life and mind. This non-dualistic view of the relation of the human and the natural is the basis of the interpretation of the divine devel-oped by Shailer Mathews. In his view, the inclusion of human per-sonality in nature which is necessitated by evolutionary thought must be allowed to influence our understanding of nature itself.

> The vital issue [in the interpretation of nature] is whether the universe in which we live as persons has any power to produce us as persons. If, as we must say in the light of science, a negative answer is logically absurd, the pattern with which we describe our relations with a cosmic ultimate must include our experience as living persons.[21]

"If we once admit that human beings are the outcome of the cosmic process we can safely argue that there are forces within it which are capable of evolving them."[22] For "humanity is organic to the uni-verse, and . . . the universe cannot be understood if humanity is abstracted from it, and the value-producing capacity of the cosmic activities in human relations ignored."[23] The universe must be seen to include activities which generate and sustain life and personality, since the universe "must be capable of producing what it has pro-duced."[24] Without this manifest capacity to support life and per-sonality, the universe would be different from what it clearly is. Therefore, nature must include activities capable of giving rise to human life and its values.

> The mysterious process which we roughly call evolution brought human-ity into being. But if that be the case, then there must be activities within the cosmos sufficient to account for the evolution of the human species with its personal qualities. There must be personality-evolving activities in the cosmos. Furthermore, these personality-evolving activities in the cosmos must continue as elements within the total environment in the midst of which we must live and to which we must be adjusted.[25]

The inclusion of human personality in nature thus automatically selects certain aspects of nature responsible for the generation and

maintenance of personality; these factors Mathews calls the personality-producing activities. That there are such personality-
producing activities in the universe is clear from the emergence of
personality and its persistence.

Mathews observes that we have developed several methods of
obtaining help from those forces upon which we are dependent. In
one of these methods, the environment is treated personally, while in
another it is impersonally manipulated and coerced. The first of these
methods is embodied in religion, while the second is expressed in
magic and, eventually, in technology.[26] Religion is an aspect of
humanity's total effort to make adjustment to its environment; it is
distinguished from other aspects of this effort by its attitude or
approach: "religion can be described as a phase of the life process
which seeks by control or co-operation to get help from those elements
of its cosmic environment upon which we feel ourselves dependent
by setting up social, that is, personal relations with them."[27] Thus
Mathews defines religion as the extending of methods discovered in
social experience to relations with nature. "The experience gained in
society, the ways of setting up help-gaining relationships with one's
peers and superiors, are utilized as patterns for the purpose of setting
up similar relations with the superhuman elements upon which we
feel ourselves dependent."[28]

This distinctive approach of religion to the issues of life is justified in practice, in that it is found to constitute the most adequate
adjustment to the personality-producing activities of nature.

> Religion is the attempt to utilize our experience as persons in setting up
> relations with these personality-producing forces. That is to say, we act
> toward the process in the midst of which we are as we act toward the
> human environment in which we are. Experience in the latter becomes the
> pattern for adjustment of ourselves to the former. . . . The individual is in
> personal relation with those personality-evolving elements of an envi-
> roning process as he or she is to society.[29]

This extension of the attitudes appropriate to personal relations to
experience as a whole is validated in its actual fruitfulness in living,
and becomes misleading only when the imagery developed in religious practice is reified and taken literally, creating a conflict with
our knowledge of the world.

The means used in the religions for bringing people into relation
with the personality-producing activities is the concept of the divine.

The purpose of the various ideas of the divine is "to integrate human life with those elements of the known universe capable of satisfying personal needs."[30] God is

> our conception, born of social experience, of the personality-evolving and personally responsive elements of our cosmic environment with which we are organically related.[31]

> The idea of God is the outcome of the effort which we have made by the use of personal experience to gain help from those elements of the environment upon which we feel ourselves dependent, and with which we attempt personal relations as instinctively as we breathe or protect our life.[32]

The concept of the divine is thus an instrument in the orientation of persons to their environment; it is "a conception born of personal experience with human persons by which the adjustment of humanity with cosmic personality-producing activity is furthered."[33]

Traditionally, the term God is taken as denoting a supernatural person, but in reality the concept of God is "an anthropomorphic conception of those personality-producing activities of the universe with which humanity is organically united."[34] Thus a distinction must be made between the actual function of concepts of the divine in relating us to the personality-producing activities, and particular contents given to them. The concept of the divine is a means for the adjustment of persons to their inclusive environment, and this function remains constant through the many particular forms the concept takes.

> Though the content of the word God may be subject to social permutation, the personal organic relationship of humanity with environing activities as established by the use of some coordinating personal pattern, is as real as our relationship with things of sense.[35]

Various patterns, such as that of King or Father, are given to the concept of the divine, each reflecting the social conditions and the state of knowledge of the time in which it was formed. The tension between a changing social experience and inherited concepts of God may lead to the development of new patterns relevant to the new experience. At present, Mathews points out, traditional patterns reflecting feudal society, patriarchal families, and an outmoded science are undergoing criticism, to the extent that many people urge the abandonment of theism itself. Against this view, Mathews asserts that even granting the inadequacy of traditional concepts of the divine, the function performed by the patterns remains important. Some means of relating to the personality-producing processes is required, and if present concepts of God are inadequate, new ones should be developed.[36] We recognize this as the program of the religious liberal.

Although the patterns constituting the content of inherited ideas of the divine are, in the light of present social experience and knowledge, inadequate and literally false, the concept of the divine expresses a concrete relation of persons and nature. Apparently, the various symbols for the divine are capable of expressing our relation to the personality-producing factors, and more importantly, of creating in us those receptive attitudes which constitute the best adjustment to these activities, quite apart from their literal falsity. The symbols for the divine are instruments rather than descriptions; they function to relate us to important realities rather than to give us information about them. The concept of God does not denote an observable entity, but symbolizes a relationship and evokes an attitude, and in this way facilitates an adjustment to the personality-producing activities. The divine is "an instrumental concept by which is furthered that reciprocal adjustment with cosmic activities which it is the aim of every religion to establish."[37]

Even though concepts of the divine do not describe the nature of the activities to which they seek to relate us, they are justified because they point toward these realities and establish relationships to them; they are not merely empty images. The divine "expresses a reality because it expresses and furthers the relation between existences."[38] In short, the idea of God expresses the relevance of nature to the values of personality without specifying the precise character of the relevant aspects of nature. Mathews terms this a "conceptual theism," because the concept of the divine as the personality-producing factors does not denote or describe these factors, but evokes that personal posture in us which is requisite to a functional relationship with them. For this reason, various patterns of the concept of the divine can function effectively, although they are literally false and contradictory. For the divine is a symbol and not a definition, and although it is subject to rational elaboration, it is primarily evocative of a certain attitude and spiritual stance. And since its function is to bring about a sensitivity to nature's responsiveness to personal life, it is to be expected that the use of personal symbolism will continue even when the literal meaning of the symbols is rejected.

In Mathews' view, the personality-producing activities are not a supernatural individual, as in traditional theism; for him concepts of the supernatural and a spiritual realm would represent a break in the coherence of reality. Thus Mathews' naturalistic theism involves the personal relationship to factors which lack personality, and even individuality. This relationship is possible, in his opinion, when nature is considered not as mechanical, but as organismic; viewed in this way, its events are seen to have the significance of fostering personal life rather than giving rise to it accidentally. This is not to say that nature is to be considered as simply friendly to humanity, or as ruled by the purpose of producing human life. It is simply that natural processes have significance as the context of personal life, which is a revelation of some of nature's powers and potentials, and that nature is sufficiently hospitable to enable the realization of personal values. While an anthropocentric view of the universe is not justified, neither is the mechanistic view; but experience does justify that personal attitude toward nature in which nature is seen as in some ways responsive to the fulfillment of persons.

The personality-producing activities include human society, but society is not to be seen as a substitute for the more inclusive process which produced and sustains it, and of which it is a part. Personal life depends upon social relationships, but society itself is an expression of the personality-producing character of nature.[39] At the same time, the personality- producing activities are not to be conceived as a discrete, distinguishable force.

> When we speak of the personality-producing activities of the universe we are not thinking of a distinguishable force like that of electricity but of that recognizable process in which the potencies of ultimate reality find expression in trends which, at least on our earth, emerge as human beings. Such a personality-producing trend is an expression of a cosmic totality discernible in successive stages in its development. The emergence of human personality from the cosmos presupposes other stages in which it is potentially but not actually present.[40]

Mathews means by the divine this potential of nature to create and sustain personal life. He refrains from what he regards as unfounded metaphysical speculation as to the ultimate nature of the activities that function in this way. We cannot fully specify those aspects of nature upon which personal life depends, but we can indicate the major prerequisite to a fruitful relationship with these factors. This is the attitude of openness to the participation of the cosmos in human efforts,[41] the spiritual stance I will refer to as "openness to gifts," an awareness of nature's grace.

In this connection, Mathews says that prayer uses personal symbolism to create an attitude of sensitivity to nature's responsiveness, and it is therefore a means of organizing the relationship with the personality-producing factors on the analogy of personal communication. Thus, prayer may establish the conditions of the growth of personality. Similarly, he defines morality as that behavior established through trial and error which is adaptive to the personality-producing activities of the universe. According to Mathews, this is the meaning of the traditional notion that God is love. This is not the projection of human personality onto the universe, but a statement of the experimentally discovered best adjustment to those cosmic activities supportive of human fulfillment.[42]

Mathews' criticism of humanism is that it substitutes isolated human effort for co-operation with those activities which actually create and fulfill human life. Humanism is "the earnest effort to substitute human endeavor for human cooperation with the forces which have made humanity possible."[43] In most forms, humanism fails to embody that openness to the creativity of nature which is necessary to the growth of the personal, since it approaches nature in the manipulative mode. But Mathews claims that the central concerns of humanism and theism converge in naturalistic theism.[44]

By definition, if the divine is conceived as those aspects of nature upon which the good of human life depends, it is not the source of evil. But the fact of evil remains, and it may be asked, why may we not introduce a concept of the demonic which selects those aspects of nature embodying resistance and obstruction to the growth of good? Mathews' response to this question is that the impersonal and anti-personal factors in nature are not personally responsive; thus, they can be personified only poetically. The proper relation to the personality-producing processes is an openness and an expectancy of unpredictable initiative; that is, a personal attitude. But the proper relation to the destructive factors is the manipulative mode, which involves the use of effort and technique to over-come them.[45]

Openness to Gifts

The two forms of naturalistic theism sketched above elaborate a concept of the divine from the point of view of human welfare, and each defines the divine as those aspects of nature upon which the good depends. These two characteristics included in the definition of naturalistic theism above suggest that naturalistic theism mediates between pantheism and humanism, the other interpretations of the divine available within naturalism. To the Chicago Naturalists, the divine is neither nature, nor the human ideal and our efforts to embody it, but nature insofar as it is supportive of human good. We might say that Ames and Mathews use the divine as a generic term; it denotes unspecified factors functioning in a characteristic way.

Ames had described the concept of idealized reality as a "concrete universal" rather than a "mere class concept," using as an example the contrast between "people" and "city." "People" is a term for a miscellaneous collection, but while "city" is also a term for a collection of individuals, they are taken to work together in a certain way to produce a result not manifest in the constituents taken separately. The divine is thus an order of events within nature so constituted as to function together to produce a consistent effect. The divine is whatever in nature contributes to this effect, and the fact that Ames conceives of the factors so indicated as a coordinated process rather than a miscellaneous collection does not alter the fact that the divine in his usage is a generic term for factors which remain unidentified, save in their consistent effect.

Similarly, Mathews' view of the divine as the personality-producing activities is a generic concept. Mathews had actually characterized his view as "conceptual theism." The divine is the concept through which we relate to unspecified activities known only in their function of fostering personal values. In describing both of these conceptions of the divine as generic in form, I am not implying that they are mere empty terms; each refers to operative realities. The point is simply that the precise nature of the factors denoted by the term *God* is not specified. The divine is whatever functions to sustain human life and its fulfillment.

The human importance claimed for these generic conceptions of the divine is that they inculcate attitudes necessary to the growth of good. In Ames' view, the notion of the divine as idealized reality fosters an optimistic frame of mind in which human effort is seen as cooperation and participation with certain tendencies of nature, rather than as lonely and heroic toil in an alien environment. In Mathews' view, the idea of the divine as the personality-producing activities encourages a personal openness, sensitivity, and feeling of relatedness to the cosmos which renders experience a means of the growth of personality. Each would likely claim that without such a concept, we might overlook the silent helpfulness of surrounding processes, or erroneously regard nature as the passive object of our domination and control. In both cases a generic concept of the divine is thought to function in religious living to produce the most fruitful orientation to experience, that orientation which we have called above the theistic stance or openness to gifts.

Wieman's approach to naturalistic theism will be sketched in the following chapters. Discussion of Ames and Mathews first does not imply any priority of their thought to his. This is a conceptual study not an historical one, and the thought of Wieman's less well-known colleagues is used here as an introduction to the novelty of naturalistic theism.

Wieman's naturalistic reinterpretation of the idea of the divine begins with the acceptance of the generic definition of the divine as those natural processes upon which human life depends. The development of his thought is driven by his growing belief that the generic concepts of the divine we have seen above are insufficient. We will see that he attempts to identify a particular "structured event" as the divine. In his writings of the 'thirties it is called "progressive integration" or "creative synthesis," a recurrent pattern discovered throughout the pre-human universe and in human life; in his later writings it is called "the creative event" or "creative interchange," a certain type of communication between persons. In these formulations he is trying to go beyond the generic conception of nature's grace and to specify that factor in nature upon which human fulfillment rests.[46]

Wieman believed that these more specific concepts communicate more than the notion that the growth of the good is related to certain tendencies in nature; they are attempts to make clear the conditions under which the creativity of nature operates in human experience. For example, in his later works Wieman hoped that the concept of creative communication would give actual knowledge of the divine which could function as a guide in decision-making in a way that the generic conception of the divine cannot. For the vague idea of openness to forces beyond our control, Wieman substitutes action to set up conditions in social life under which creative interchange between persons may occur. A central claim in this study of Wieman's naturalistic theism will be that his thought is driven by this desire for increasing specificity about the nature of the divine creative activity.

But precisely because Wieman tries to become more specific about the factors in nature which support and fulfill human life, his views will become more vulnerable to criticism. It may be that the concept of creative communication which we will encounter in later chapters is not able to bear the weight which Wieman places upon it. If the particular form of social psychology on which this concept is based is questioned, then the underlying sense of dependence upon nature's powers and processes may also be lost. And it may be that this is what is most important about naturalistic theism, because the central issue among religious naturalists was the choice between two different approaches to life, the Promethean stance of humanism and the theistic stance. So despite their differences, the fundamental insight of the Chicago Naturalists would seem to be that however dubious and historically limited traditional concepts of God may be, grace is quite real. Indeed, nature includes grace.

Chapter Two

Creative Synthesis

The vital core of Wieman's naturalistic theism is found in his writings of the period 1929–1938. We will encounter what I take to be the less estimable earlier and the more problematic later work in the next chapter. Half a century after the publication of these texts of his middle period, the reader is at first struck by the oddness of their purpose and vocabulary. Here we read of an operational concept of God, the testing of religious ideas through observation of their consequences, experimental religious living, naturalistic theism, worshipful autosuggestion, and problem-solving mysticism. We are puzzled by the peculiarity of the attempt to think about God as an observable process within the natural world, and by the singularity of this combination of empiricist methodology and concern for practical religious life. This seeming oddness is the result of Wieman's earnest, perhaps even single-minded, concern to deal with the problems created for theology by science, problems which have not been dealt with forthrightly by the style of theology dominant since his time. Wieman desires to give concrete content to the idea of divine grace, portraying it as an experienceable reality observed to operate in tangible ways in nature and human life.

Our study of Wieman's naturalistic concept of God thus begins with his writings of the 'thirties (works listed in the bibliography as written between 1929 and 1938). Prior to this, up to *The Wrestle of Religion with Truth* (1927), Wieman had expressed his empiricist concern for a concept of God as an experienceable reality, but in that book he merely offered an interpretation of the so-called "principle of concretion" adapted from the philosophy of Alfred North Whitehead (1861–1947). Wieman evidently became aware of the lack of fit between an empiricist methodology and this element borrowed from Whitehead's metaphysical system, and so in subsequent writings he set about developing his own concept of the divine creative activity. Here he elaborated his theistic naturalism as a vision of the tendency in nature and human life toward the making of relations and wholes. This phase of Wieman's thought is the most interesting and suggestive. But then, in what is surely his best known and most technical book, *The Source of Human Good* (1946), he seems to have become both more doubtful of our ability to speak of the cosmic scope of creativity, and at the same time interested in being more specific about the way the divine creativity actually works in human experience. As a result, in his later writings he speaks almost exclusively of "the creative event" as a type of human communication. And so it is to the middle period of Wieman's work which we now turn.

An Empirical Approach to The Divine Creative Activity

Wieman seems to be in the position of many of us who have come to question the truth or value of the concept of the supernatural God, but who retain a sense of the reality and presence of grace in human life. He says that the truth of traditional symbols of religious devotion is no longer clear because they lack authentication by the method through which science and common sense test and prove ideas. For Wieman, this is the rational-empirical method as interpreted in American pragmatism, in which ideas are valued as true if they are observed to have the power to guide our action successfully. Wieman believed that in the past, religious symbols and ritual inculcated attitudes which brought people into relation with healing and sustaining power, but that now these same ideas have lost their hold on the imagination. Taken as beliefs about the supernatural, they seem untestable in experience and therefore empty. What is required is a concept of the divine creative activity which generates practices that bring us into relation with observable events and processes. Of course, human action and observation of consequences are confined to the natural world, while statements about what is thought to be beyond nature cannot be tested, and so the method Wieman adopts leads to a theistic naturalism, a concept of God as a creativity immanent in nature.

Since for Wieman the only reality of God knowable is that encountered in the consequences of our action, speculative ideas about God as transcendent ground or source of the world are regarded as misleading; they turn us away from the proximate to the remote and blind us to "the divine significance of immediate reality."[1] Thus, for example, while Wieman commends W.E. Hocking for his notion of the "Whole Idea" as a system of supportive interrelations underlying human life, he rejects as speculative and untestable the suggestion that this is an all-inclusive divine mind. The claim that reality is mind leads to no particular predictable consequences, and thus it cannot be confirmed or disconfirmed by any particular state of affairs. However, he is open to certain philosophical ideas of God which he feels refer to those observable processes in which interrelations grow; he mentions Jan Smuts' idea of "holism," the "nisus toward ever higher syntheses" in Samuel Alexander, and Whitehead's principle of concretion. Wieman's distrust of speculative ideas on the grounds that they are compatible with any set of observable events and, therefore, untestable probably limits his interest in Whitehead to this one aspect of the latter's larger concept of God.[2]

The Growth of Good

As an operational concept of the divine, Wieman offers the idea of "creative synthesis" or "progressive integration." He wants us to notice the subtle, persistent, recurrent tendency within nature by which relations of mutual support and mutual enhancement are woven. The universe includes a tendency to integrate diverse elements in a way that makes them increasingly interdependent, so that powers and qualities in one enter into the character of the other. In this way new wholes are formed which have capabilities and characteristics not present in the parts separately; in these organic unities the parts work to sustain the whole, and the whole sustains and enhances the parts. The growth of mutuality and interrelatedness is seen in the process which unites sub-atomic events so that they manifest the varied characters of atoms of increasing complexity, and leads on to the elaboration of molecules, living cells, many-celled organisms, sensitive organisms, minds, and historical communities of minds. Notice that in spite of the examples listed, the process of integration is not itself evolution, but only one factor within it; evolution includes many other processes involving conflict and destruction. Further, this growth is not inevitable progress, for structures of relatedness are constantly destroyed. Growth is not irresistible or omnipotent, but it is persistent; often suppressed and reversed, it springs up again and again. Wieman concludes, "God is the integrating process at work in the universe. It is that which makes for increasing interdependence and cooperation in the world."[3]

To express this idea another way, creative synthesis is the growth of value in human life.

> God is that which progressively and in greatest measure increases the value of existence. The progressive integrating process of the universe is what does this. Hence it is God.[4]

Whatever one's theory of what makes an experience good for persons, value increases if activities which are good are brought into relations by which they support and sustain each other and through which they enlarge and enhance each other. Hence the growth of connections increases the value of human experience.

Further, the growth of relations of mutual support and enhancement itself gains a new dimension in relations involving minds. In thought, one experience can "mean" another, be connected with it through association; then enjoyment of one moment is magnified by the others with which the mind associates it. In some cases this connection of meaning increases our ability to repeat enjoyments, when one experience "means" another because it is causally related to it. Thus Wieman speaks of the growth of value as the increase of "that connection between enjoyable activities by which they support, . . . enhance . . . and, at a higher level, mean one another."[5] And this growth of value is God.

> God is the *growth* of meaning and value in the world. This growth consists of increase in those connections between activities which make the activities mutually sustaining, mutually enhancing, and mutually meaningful.[6]

The growth of connections of mutual support and enhancement which is creative synthesis is superhuman but not, as far as we can see, supernatural. It is manifest as a healing and nurturing process within the human body. The physical organism grows, heals, recuperates, defends, compensates, and adapts; and all of this manifests the tendency toward growth of supportive connections, entirely apart from our knowledge and effort. The human role is merely to set the conditions necessary for growth or to remove obstacles to it, as we do in cultivating plants; but when conditions are appropriate, growth comes by a grace beyond our power. Other examples can be mentioned. The growth of mind through the accumulation of insights and perspectives from others and their integration into an expanding system increases our awareness; yet this is more than the outcome of conscious intention, for it goes beyond what we could imagine or plan on the basis of the present state of the personality. The growth of friendship and love, too, are largely unconscious; although the needed occasions and attitudes must be provided for, growth is the result of a process of interaction and mutual adaptation that could not be arranged and that leads to results we could not foresee. Growth is superhuman and not merely the work of the human mind, even when it operates in human life; the specific character of its results is unpredictable, and it occurs spontaneously when appropriate conditions are present. The concept of creative synthesis as the growth of community therefore consists in countless instances of what I have been calling nature's grace.

Creative Synthesis and God

Wieman has identified an activity observed to operate on all levels of the universe which is "a mysterious power of marvelous gentleness"[7] but which is also amazingly persistent and steadfast in the face of seemingly more powerful forces of inertia and decay. To the degree that we observe relations of mutuality to exist and grow, this process is an experienceable factor within and around us. Still, it may not be clear why this natural process should be called God. Wieman believes that creative synthesis has the value of God because it is worthy of our supreme loyalty and devotion, as that which creates, sustains, and fulfills human life. Our existence as living organisms is a gift dependent upon a matrix of supportive connections elaborated through a long evolution. Our personalities as growing systems of interconnected meanings, attitudes, values, and habits are instances of the grace of creative synthesis. It is creative synthesis which transforms our minds in unanticipated ways when we are open to its promptings, so that we transcend present limitations and experience the qualitative richness of the world more fully, and relate to its supportive energies more adequately. Finally, progressive integration works to increase human interdependence, modifying behavior to render it more cooperative and mutually helpful when we are adapted to it, creating that form of living community in which human life is fulfilled. Thus "God is . . . this actual, existing, operative reality in our midst bringing forth all that is highest and best in existence, far beyond the scope of our specific understanding, . . . the creative synthesis at work in the immediate concrete situation where we are."[8]

In naturalistic theism, God is seen as that which rightly commands devotion, the source of good; Wieman rejects the contrasting approach which defines God as the source of all existence. "God is not the creator, meaning the mysterious source of everything. God is only the source of good."[9] In Wieman's empiricism we cannot know anything about the ultimate source of the world. The universe as a whole supports both good and evil, and so is "characterless" from the point of view of concern for human good, as would be its maker; thus neither nature nor a supernatural creator would be worthy of worship. "Since one essential criterion of God is 'greatest power for good,' and since clear thinking shows that such a power for good cannot be the total universe, nor the creator of everything, it becomes plain that God must be something in the universe, namely that something which exercises greatest power for good."[10] Such a God is one tendency within nature among many. "God is within the cosmic whole, . . . one part of it."[11] Progressive synthesis is widely operative, but it is not dominant over the universe nor is it the purpose of the universe as a whole; not all phases of the universe grow toward integration, and the universe cannot be said to be dominated by any one purpose. Thus, theistic naturalism is not pantheism, nor is it panentheism; God is not nature as a whole or its essential structure, as in Spinoza; and nature is not included within God and thus pervaded by the divine influence, as in Hartshorne. Rather, God is included within nature as one activity, and not the dominant one; yet this activity is the source of life and its further development.

Since the creative source of good is not the cause of the universe as a whole, there would seem in naturalistic theism to be no problem of evil; that is, Wieman obviates the problem which the fact of evil poses for belief in divine goodness and omnipotence by denying that God is omnipotent. His God is, then, a finite God. But the undeniable fact of evil raises questions of another sort for naturalistic theism: does progressive integration sometimes do evil? Is synthesis ever evil? Are there not evils of growth?

Wieman believes that the growth of relations of mutuality is always in itself an increase of value, although humans may use the resulting increase of perception or power in destructive ways. Evil is whatever opposes creative synthesis; thus, while synthesis itself is not evil, the results of its past operation may become so. The important distinction here is that between the process of integration, which is always creative of value, and the existing structures of integration, which become evil when they block the way toward richer, more intense integrations. And notice that this is the fundamental distinction made in all forms of theism between that which is creative and that which it has created. Existing goods must be sacrificed for emerging good, in which more diverse elements are included, or in which there will be a greater degree of mutual support and enhancement. This shows that the growth of relatedness involves conflict and destruction, and may call for sacrifice and relinquishing. Sometimes the growth of richer, more intense integrations involves the loss of present orders; so the God of creative synthesis is also a destroyer, at times "wrathful." Wieman even asserts that perhaps humanity will be destroyed for the sake of the growth of good.

The evils of growth are those forms of growth which are defensive responses to threats. Here an individual grows so as to preserve itself by blocking and warding-off influences from others. Instances of this use of structure to prevent further change and deeper relatedness are the shell, bark, or rind; armor and military organization; domination of others and ego defenses; and rigid social conventions and schemes of orthodoxy. These forms of organization are attempts to diminish connection and prevent the emergence of the new. In contrast with this form of growth, the creative response to threats is to yield oneself to transformation; here Wieman expresses an insight central to both Buddhism and Christianity. Thus, the evil type of growth is "competitive growth," which is a lack of and resistance to "organic growth." Again, whatever obstructs growth of the organic sort must be broken, transformed, sacrificed, or eliminated, whether it is a species, an institution, or a habit.

Wieman was often asked if there is a source of evil, a naturalistic counterpart to the concept of Satan. He maintained that evil has no single definable character common to all its forms. It is simply a miscellany of factors whose only link is that they oppose progressive synthesis, whereas good has a unique, identifiable character involving the emergence of mutually supportive connections. Some evil works to destroy relations without building more comprehensive ones, other evil is simply the absence of them, while still another form involves the fixation of existing structures in a posture of resistance to transformation and emergence. Unlike good, evil has no common character, and thus no single source.

Is the Finite God Transcendent and Personal?

It is becoming clear that Wieman's naturalistic theism portrays God as a temporal process within the natural world, with persistent but limited power. Is Wieman's God transcendent in any sense? First, as we have seen, creative synthesis is at work in transformations of the human mind beyond its present scope, bringing about what we could not imagine or plan; thus, it is superhuman, transcendent of human knowledge and effort. All we can do is set the conditions for and remove obstacles to its functioning. We "can increase the good of life and the good of the world only as we adjust to this integrating behavior of the universe and cooperate with it."[12] Wieman was later to call this "functional transcendence;" progressive integration does for us what we cannot do for ourselves.

This notion can be amplified by recalling that progressive integration is a ceaseless striving for new, more inclusive networks of relation. Thus we might say, secondly, that transcendence is present in Wieman's world through the concept of the future; Wieman is enraptured by the vision of the infinite range of possibilities which creative synthesis may actualize, the vast unimaginable openness of a growing universe. Possibilities are not another realm beyond the one world of nature for Wieman, and they do not require a divine mind to house them, as in Whitehead's thought. According to naturalism, they are genuine constituents of the world, *in* things as their potential transformations. Wholeness of personality, clearness of mind, a just society, and mutual understanding are possible perfectings of self and society, latent within them, just as life and consciousness are realizations of potentialities in matter.

According to Wieman, the world as presently experienced is a "social construct" based on the interests and perspectives developed within a particular group. There is a wider reality waiting to be perceived, as our minds are transformed by the inclusion of new interests and perspectives. "We are folded in the encompassing presence of great beauty and love which cannot enter . . . consciousness" on the basis of the present state of the self and society.[13] This is shown in the ability of the artist to experience and disclose overlooked qualities in the world, in the ability of some persons to elicit an open, kindly response where we could not, and in our own experience of having our sensibilities awakened and the world thereby transfigured. There is a more richly textured reality to be experienced, and yet this greater world is the hidden depth of the one world of nature.

The infinite extent of possible transformations reaches beyond changes in human life and constitutes a form of transcendence in Wieman's thought, although he does not speak in this way. But when we ask if God transcends the natural world, Wieman usually seems to reply negatively. All of our interactions take place in the world of events, and our testable knowledge is limited to that world. Usually Wieman speaks as if creative synthesis exhausts the concept of the divine. He sometimes asks if we might say that God is actually an eternal, changeless order beyond nature; in that case, the observable process in which mutuality grows would be a partial manifestation of this order within the temporal world. Wieman replies in these writings of the 'thirties that we may speak this way as long as we remember that this is merely one possible, untestable idea, and that as psycho-physical organisms we encounter God only as a process within nature.[14] This concession to tradition and metaphysics was to become more muted and grudging in his later works.

Since Wieman speaks of the process of integration as God, we must ask not only about transcendence, but about personality. In Wieman's naturalistic theism God is not a person, but the source of personality; the divine could not be the source of personality if it were itself limited to being a mere person. Wieman feels that what makes personality possible is a complex, ever-changing matrix of connections which is elaborated and maintained by countless events of integration; this system of relations includes inorganic events, complex interactions of living organisms and their sustaining environment, and those processes within human communities in which meanings are communicated through symbols. Personality depends on this vast matrix, built up through eons, reconstructed and maintained moment by moment through progressive synthesis; thus, God must be much more than a personality in order to create it. Wieman insists that we must accept the results of inquiry regarding the source of personality, and renounce both our craving for a cosmic companion and the egoistic assumption that that which is of greatest value must be like us.

> God, then, is not a personality, but God is more worthful than any personality could ever be. God is not nature and . . . is not the universe, but is the growth of living connections of value in the universe. If one wishes one can say this is not God but is the work of God. Practically, it comes to the same thing.[15]

Here Wieman portrays God as observably at work in the world of natural events, wholly immanent and temporal, and as the impersonal source of human personality and its fulfillment.

The Instrumental Character of the Concept of God

What does Wieman think about the nature and status of his concept of creative synthesis? Does it represent, for example, the discovery of a force or ingredient in the universe? I think Wieman would answer this last question negatively.

Progressive integration is an observed behavior, a trait of the universe, and not an occult force causing the integrations we observe; it is the *fact* of synthesis, and not the reason for it. To hypostatize it would be to commit the error of speculative metaphysics, which is to transform abstractions invented to describe observed behavior into unseen realities thought to underlie what we observe. "God, the progressive integrating process, is the movement toward richer and more intensive integrations,"[16] and I interpret this statement to mean that what has the value of the divine is the *movement* and not the hidden *mover*. This is an operational or instrumental concept (to use the terminology of the pragmatists, who have influenced Wieman), just as some would say that gravity is not an occult force moving objects, but a name for the fact that they move in a certain way.

The influence of pragmatism on Wieman is seen in the fact that he is skeptical of the ability of any idea or system of ideas to grasp the nature of reality; concepts are guides in our interaction with our environment and not disclosures of its inner being. But Wieman's stated reasons for metaphysical skepticism in this period of his thought are derived from his process view of nature. Ironically, he rejects the metaphysical systems of Whitehead and Hartshorne in the name of some aspects of their process vision of reality. He gives these reasons for his belief that no thought system can capture the ultimate nature of reality: (1) the richness of the world, which constantly reveals itself to be more intricate than we imagined or were able to anticipate; (2) the unpredictability of emergent changes; (3) the ineffable nature of the qualities we encounter in immediate experience; (4) the limitation of every interpretation of reality to one socially-determined perspective; (5) the fact that new knowledge flows from every new technique of inquiry; (6) the extreme and fundamental character of the changes nature undergoes through the eons.[17] What I am calling Wieman's fourth reason for skepticism regarding philosophy's claim to be able to grasp the nature of reality, he attributes to Karl Mannheim's sociology of knowledge; all of the others except the third have counterparts in Whitehead (although they did not lead Whitehead to an anti-metaphysical conclusion). Surely this strand in Wieman's thought qualifies Wieman for the encomium "post-modern;" that is, he shares with late twentieth-century thought the belief that reason is an interpretation from the human perspective of a mysterious, shifting environment, and is not a supernatural faculty with the power to penetrate into the ultimate nature of reality. So the concept of God merely operates to place us in relation with a creativity it cannot capture.

It is clear why Wieman distrusts all concepts of God, including his own. They blind us to unfathomable complexity and give us narrow expectations which make us imperceptive of novelty; they become idolatrous substitutes for that to which they point. Our allegiance must not be to a particular idea of God, according to Wieman, but to that reality which exceeds every concept of it. This much can be said by the symbolic theory of religious language elaborated by

Paul Tillich and others in recent theology. But Wieman goes on. The only justification for ideas of God (or of anything else) is that they direct our attention and guide our action, and this is something Tillich's "symbols of transcendent mystery" do not do in the way that "creative synthesis" does, because the latter refers to observable events. Wieman says we are to treat the idea of God as progressive integration as an operational idea; that is, it is shaped to guide behavior and not to inform us about the nature of reality, telling us what to look for rather than informing us about the underlying cause of what we see. And as such, it is subject to revision in the light of observed consequences of that behavior which it purports to guide, for our loyalty is not to the idea but to the process to which it relates us.

Faith as Commitment to Constant Transformation

Faith in God as progressive synthesis would be commitment to constant transformation by its influence, entrusting our lives to unforeseen growth. In this we yield up the present order of our lives, open ourselves to influences which may lead to new connections, and await unpredictable changes that will grow within us and around us. Wieman especially stresses the need for willingness to sacrifice existing good, itself the work of creative synthesis in the past, for the sake of emerging good. "Every form of existence must perish in order that further possibilities of meaning and value may be realized."[18] Wieman understands the biblical irony that good people, customs, and institutions are the greatest barriers to the growth of good. "Every specific organization of existence is an obstacle to the realization of further possibilities."[19] After any new order of self or society is elaborated, our hold on it must be loosened; the commitment that is faith is directed to the process of creative synthesis and not its products, to the creator and not the created. Lack of faith would be in part a fear which defends itself from influences working for change and which clings to and defends present structures.

This view of faith as trust in creative synthesis and openness to the changes it brings leads us to a deeper understanding of Wieman's definition of God as the source of human good. The divine creative activity does not simply fulfill our present wants and realize our present conception of what would be good; rather, it transforms us in unanticipated ways so that our conception of the good changes. Creative synthesis functions in Wieman's thought as the norm of human good; while we may resist and cling to present good, the working of creative synthesis reveals that the good of human life is constant transformation.

Faith understood in this way gives the power to accept loss, failure, suffering, and disaster because while we savor and value present good, we are not to cling to it; we are able to accept the perishing of all of the structures of value in our lives without loss of hope, for faith is "absolute self-commitment to unlimited connective growth even when it threatens to destroy" the individual.[20] The other side of this yieldedness, this sense of present good as inadequate beside the infinitely rich possibilities of growth, is positive awareness of the capacity of persons and situations for endless transformation; there is a longing for the richer experience of which we are capable, an expectancy and alertness for intimations of the new.

Implied in this definition of faith as the mark of the religious way of living is a criticism of secular idealism, which is especially important since most American naturalists were religious humanists in the pattern of John Dewey. To Wieman, humanism is devotion to the best ideals discoverable within the present structure of consciousness. A moral ideal or a plan of social reform is a possibility which is within our power to bring into existence and reflects personal, class, and historical bias; humanism is simply the direction of intelligence and effort toward the realization of present ideals. The religious approach to life, in contrast, senses that the greatest good is opposed to the prevailing order of thought; it comes about through a process which works beyond human power and brings about new ideals and orders which we could not imagine or seek. We cannot be open to newly emerging value if we look only for what would fulfill existing plans and ideals. As opposed to moralistic effort to improve oneself or build a better world according to an existing plan, faith in creative synthesis is not willful and intense, but relaxed and expectant, open to emerging good. The mark of the uniquely religious approach to life is acceptance of the need for constant transformation, readiness for the redirection of life beyond present purposes.

Methods of Religious Living

Just as Wieman feels it necessary to present an empirical concept of
the divine creativity because of the decline of traditional symbols,
similarly he offers methods developed in "experimental living"
which he believes will do for modern people what prayer and worship have always done. Wieman is a theological realist; prayer and
worship are not merely means of effecting subjective states, but are
ways of bringing about a relationship between persons and a real
source of change. Prayer establishes an attitude of openness to a creativity "rooted deep in the cosmic process"[21] that brings about
growth in subtle and unconscious ways in the self and between it
and supportive factors in the situation. Of course, the specific words
of prayer are not directed to creativity, but to oneself and other wor-
shipers, and their effect is on personal attitudes; but when these attitudes establish a relation to creativity, the resulting growth is the
work of God.

The belief that human action merely sets the conditions for the
mysterious process of growth is seen in Wieman's use of the term
worshipful autosuggestion for this method of solitary meditation; in
this process, conscious method establishes receptivity to a source of
change which is more than human intention.

The method, to be practiced at regular intervals and in a secluded
place, involves five steps. (1) We are to relax and become aware of
that upon which human life and its fulfillment depend, which is the
living, growing matrix of organic relations, the "encompassing and
sustaining and integrating reality which is called God."

(2) Then we are to "call to mind the vast, unimaginable possibilities for good inherent in this integrating process."[22] This must not
involve a concept of specific states of affairs because we cannot know
on the basis of the present organization of our attitudes and relationships what the best sort of change would be; we merely invoke
a sense of undefined possibilities which may be actualized through
creative synthesis.

(3) Next we must face a specific and important problem or conflict in life; if we are seriously undertaking responsibilities, risking
difficulties, open to the suffering of others, aware of the profounder
community which is undeveloped in every friendship, an issue will
readily come to mind.

(4) Self-analysis follows, in which we are to search for changes which must be made in attitudes and patterns. It sounds at first as if we are to plan some sort of rearrangement in ourselves, but Wieman believes that if the first two steps have set a mood of self-relinquishment and openness to the new, a novel possibility will emerge intuitively through our coming into relation with "the constructing, uplifting, life-giving, integrating process of the world."[23] In this method, we seek to align ourselves so as to serve as links enabling the integrating process at work in the universe to complete itself.

(5) Lastly, we should formulate concisely the readjustment required in order to relate the disconnected processes in the situation; since we seek to establish a connection, the statement should be affirmative. In dealing with the problem of egoism and concern for prestige in a particular situation, we might say, "I enter into deep community of heart and mind with . . ." or "I am simple, lowly, sensitive, and sympathetic toward. . . ." This is, of course, autosuggestion, a concept which had been used by humanists interested in a naturalistic or reductive explanation of the power of prayer. What is interesting in Wieman's approach is his linking of autosuggestion with a source of transformation beyond and beneath conscious effort; Wieman's view of meditation is not a form of self-manipulation but is based in theological realism.

A second method practiced by Wieman he called *problem-solving mysticism*. Again we see the odd combination of instrumentalist practicality and worshipful self-relinquishment. This method is relevant when we encounter impossibility, when a solution cannot be found by combining existing ideas or responding in customary ways; the problem requires a new integration of the data of experience, a new way of interpretation or response.

We must have earnestly struggled with the problem using available ideas and methods and discovered their inadequacy. We must have a rich store of experience and thought, perhaps from immersion in the literature or lore of a religious tradition, or from habitual conversation with a circle of intimates about things that matter.

Then we must wait, without formulated thought, in receptivity and responsiveness, without a preconception of what we are waiting for. This may remind the reader of Martin Heidegger's "meditative thinking" as "waiting which is not awaiting or waiting-for."[24] Wieman explains the function of this waiting by referring to the experience of the solution of a problem popping into mind just when we have set the problem aside. This is an instance of what Viktor Frankl calls "paradoxical intention," in which "hyperintention" prevents the solution of a problem, and the goal is reached only when the attempt to reach it is abandoned.[25] This state of mental formlessness is not a blank mind because one is aware of the problem and under stimulation by it; the mind is alert, but not at work manipulating ideas.

Wieman believes that this state constitutes openness to God, adjustment to creative synthesis; this waiting "in mystic quietude" for a more adequate integration of experience to arise is the theistic stance, the posture of worship. It is precisely the opposite of self-reliant problem solving. Yet out of this openness, Wieman believes, will often come the solution to a problem. Thus problem-solving mysticism "consists in exposing oneself to the stimulus of a problematical situation with a mind free of all bias and preconception, and waiting in this state, or returning periodically to it, until there dawns upon the mind that integration which will solve the problem."[26]

In another context Wieman described what he called *the method of religious living*. (1) The method begins in the experience of crisis. According to Wieman, fundamental to our nature is the desire for a more abundant life, a consciousness in which we are responsive to a wider and deeper range of reality in nature, other persons, and ourselves; but this need is obscured by short-sighted preoccupation with specific goods and immediate problems. An experience of crisis may interrupt our activity so that we sense that the way we are living is unsatisfactory in the light of our deepest need.

(2) The adequate response to crisis Wieman calls decision. Rather than seek a way out of the crisis, we should consciously commit ourselves to "the growth of good" as the increase of mutually supportive connections as opposed to the pursuit of particular goods and definable objectives. We are to pledge to seek the best in every situation, knowing that it is more than we can anticipate or intend.

(3) We should next practice what Wieman calls release. We are to let go of present goals and concerns so as not to be limited by them; we thereby become open to new insights.

(4) The next movement is termed specification. This is in effect the emergence of new intentions; we should become clear about what we must do, obtain, learn, or remove so that our relations will be more enriching. The reader may respond that if we knew what is required and could state it, we would not have experienced a crisis of dissatisfaction in the first place. But recall that Wieman believes that if we have entered into that openness that is worship, a new pattern not within the reach of intentional, problem-solving thought will emerge. It will do so because the mind as a system of interconnected meanings has been built up through progressive integration and is subject to transformation by it when we arrange the proper conditions.

(5) The final phase is called fellowship. Wieman feels that religious life requires the support of a small group of persons meeting regularly in such a way that mutual knowledge and trust arise among the members; these groups of six to twelve people are the focus of the church's "saving, transforming power." The reason for this is that the primary way in which creative synthesis works in human life is through "shared meaning" (a term derived from Dewey), "creative interaction," or "creative synthesis of perspectives."[27] In a certain sort of communication, new ways of sensing and responding pass from one person to another, and as they are integrated into the mind, our experience of the world is broadened and deepened. Wieman expanded this concept in his later work into the idea of creative interchange, in the quest for greater specificity about the working of creativity.

Theological Realism and Worship

This notion of the expansion of the mind through shared meaning is related to the way Wieman treats the question of how prayer is "answered." Wieman insists that religious life yields tangible results, and he is constantly critical of the modern tendency to reduce religion to the merely subjective. Remember that Wieman believes that there is much of the natural world which does not enter present experience; the world that is registered in conscious appreciation is a selection from a richer, more complex field. As our patterns of perception and interpretation change, the universe as experienced changes. For Wieman, worship is a way of changing attitudes, and it thereby changes the experienced world.

> Now worship is one way of achieving a different kind of world by chang-
> ing our way of reacting [a] so that we are sensitive to certain qualities
> which could not previously reach appreciative consciousness, [b] so that
> we do things we would not previously do and this elicits features of the
> world that were previously inaccessible to experience, [c] so that our imag-
> ination functions differently thus bringing to consciousness meanings and
> fancies and feelings that we could not before undergo.[28]

Wieman knows that attitudes are influenced by heredity and the
social environment, but he holds that we are also free to cultivate
some attitudes rather than others, and he believes that worship is
the deepest, most effective way of shaping attitudes because it opens
us to the working of creative synthesis. Note that the resulting
changes have first to do with increasing our awareness of aspects
of ourselves and our world, so that our experience is aesthetically
richer and more satisfying; this change comes about by the growth
of new ways of seeing and new ways of acting. But secondly, this
expanded awareness brings us into relation with currents and powers in the world that work upon our lives and support our efforts.
Creative synthesis is thus manifest in creating new connections of
mutual support and enhancement within the self, and between the
self and the healing, nurturing factors in the environment.

When our comportment is forced, assertive, jerky, or arbitrary, we
are limited to what we can accomplish by our own conscious effort
and cut off from those currents in the environing world and our own
organism which could support us. Wieman claims that in the worshipful attitude, we are "plastic, sensitive, and responsive"[29] in relation to subtle processes of growth and the ways the resulting new
connections can empower us and buoy us up. To use a metaphor
absent in Wieman but appropriate to his vision, when we act as if
our floating depended entirely on our own effort, as if we had to
conquer the water to remain above it, we are blocked from discovering the supportiveness of the medium and our own buoyancy
when we are at ease within it. Paradoxically, when we set aside our
intensity, our concern for achieving the result we can presently imagine, our effectiveness increases. Wieman adds that this openness to
supportive currents in the environment, healing powers in our bodies, and processes of integration in our minds is not attained once
for all, but must be maintained by the methods of religious living
described above, that is, by prayer.

Wieman's realism about the presence of a trait or behavior of nature which works beyond human knowledge and effort to fulfill human life, was developed in the midst of the debate between those naturalists who were religious humanists and the group of naturalistic theists associated with the University of Chicago. This fact underlies his treatment of autosuggestion and worship, since the former is a human initiative and the latter is openness to nature's grace. Even though he was a naturalist, Wieman stands within that tradition which stresses "the sovereignty of God and the insufficiency of human self-reliance." Daniel Day Williams referred to this trait as "Wieman's Calvinism," and it accounts for his being associated in the American theological mind of the 'thirties with the neo-supernaturalists Karl Barth and Emil Brunner as, like them, a critic of the subjectivism of many religious liberals.[30] Wieman is, in short, a theological realist.

Autosuggestion, the formulation and repetition of a new idea or attitude we hope to implant and nurture in our lives, can be used to establish any pattern of change whatsoever, including attitudes useful in the domination and manipulation of others for one's own gain. But in Wieman's view, to discover the best attitudes to adopt requires worship. Worship involves relinquishing our hold on the present order of our lives, invoking a sense of the vast range of possibilities for change, and openness to that process through which new patterns of mutually sustaining and enhancing connection are woven. In this process, we must forego desire for any particular result. Clearly, Wieman emphasized the transformation of the self rather than the achievement of presently envisaged ends. This fact might be overlooked or underemphasized because of the undeniable presence of the language of self-manipulation and autosuggestion in his writing. Autosuggestion does not itself do the work of the process called God but enables an adjustment to this process, and "when this adjustment is made, the process does the work."[31] This is the theistic attitude to life as distinct from humanism; yet it is the theistic stance without the supernatural God, because it centers on the grace within nature.

Chapter Three

Creative Interchange

We turn now to Wieman's writings of the periods before and after those discussed in the previous chapter. In his earliest attempts to formulate a naturalistic view of the divine, Wieman gave the clearest statement of some of his basic methods and insights. Yet, in retrospect, the work of this period may disappoint; its empirical method reflects a somewhat dated attempt to depict religious experience as a special foundation for religious thought, and the naturalistic concept of God supposedly derived from this method is simply a borrowed element from the speculative metaphysical vision of Whitehead. The inappropriateness of this speculative idea to his empiricist method led Wieman to the developments studied in the previous chapter. Then the drive toward ever more specific formulations of the way the divine creative activity operates in human life moved Wieman beyond the idea of creative synthesis to an exclusive emphasis on creativity in communication. As will be seen, this approach introduces new problems.

Empiricism and Religious Experience

The initial steps in the development of Wieman's concept of the divine were taken in a pair of volumes which should be seen as a single unit of thought, *Religious Experience and Scientific Method* (1926) and *The Wrestle of Religion with Truth* (1927). The first sets forth the framework of theological realism and empirical method within which Wieman was to work, and the second expands and completes the line of thought begun in the first book by proposing a specific content for the concept of God.

What I am calling Wieman's realism is seen in what appears to be a formal definition of God which is fundamental to his thought.

In a sense, the reality of the divine is established by definition for Wieman, in that God is taken to be that aspect of the universe which functions to create and sustain the greatest abundance of human life, whatever this may in fact turn out to be.

> Whatever else the word God may mean, it is a term used to designate that Something upon which human life is most dependent for its security, welfare, and increasing abundance. That there *is* such a Something cannot be doubted. The mere fact that human life happens, and continues to happen, proves that this Something, however unknown, does exist.[1]

The existence of these conditions underlying the good of human life is thus not in question; only their character remains to be specified. Wieman believes that this is the form of all traditional concepts of God; God has meant the source of human good, and to live in relation with God is to undergo growth toward the best that life can attain. Even if the particular content of traditional conceptions of God is rejected in naturalism, the greatest human good depends on some objective conditions; the naturalist cannot simply rest content with the rejection of supernaturalism, but must ask, if it is not the supernatural, personal God that fulfills human life, what is it that functions in this way? Wieman and his students had a real sense that they were conducting an inquiry designed to discover what in the world of natural events is the real power intended by traditional ideas of God. This point of departure establishes Wieman as a theological realist, despite his naturalism. God is an actual, operative character of the world, to which human adjustment must be made if life is to be fulfilled.

For Wieman, human good is satisfaction of interest, and thus according to the above definition, God is that structure of the totality of being which determines the way this totality affects human interests. The largest fulfillment of interests arises through the best adaptation between this determining structure and human life. The good of our life, as the satisfaction of interest, increases as we become responsive to a wider and fuller environment. The greatest good and the most complete fulfillment of interests would be that condition in which the person is responsive and adaptive to the widest and fullest range of being.[2]

Combining the definitions of the divine as the source of good and of good as increase of the richness of experience, Wieman proposes to use an empirical method to reach an understanding of the divine. The content of the concept of God is to be discovered in the investigation of the actual conditions on which the constant expansion of awareness depends.

From Dewey, Wieman draws the description of "the method of knowing." All knowledge arises through rational reflection on experience and the testing of the resulting inferences against future experience. "Truth consists of concepts put into the form of beliefs that can be verified by way of experimental operations."[3] This method of knowing is found in common sense and everyday practice, and it is used in specialized applications in the crafts, and in an intensified form in the sciences. Wieman's unusual proposal was that the rational-empirical-experimental method now be applied to the question of religious knowledge. Religious experience is to be examined so as to generate a concept of the divine, which can then be tested in religious practice.

Wieman shared in the widespread interest in the phenomenology of religious experience stimulated by the work of William James (1842–1910). During this period he regarded religious experience as the datum for religious thought and the basis of the empirical investigation into the nature of the divine that he proposed. But in contrast with some of the religious experience enthusiasts, Wieman claimed that there is no separate faculty of religious experience and that it is not a disclosure of another realm. Rather, religious experience is a form of sensory experience of the actual world of events, "a certain way of experiencing the world of empirical fact."[4] Religious experience is not itself knowledge but simply a pre-reflective datum; from it, reason is to derive a concept of the divine as that which functions in experience to increase human good through the expansion of awareness. When reflection derives inferences regarding the character of the divine from religious experience, these are to be tested in religious applications through "methods of religious living" like those we have already seen. For Wieman, truth involves a claim concerning the consequences of beliefs in action. If the venturesome life whose commitment is guided by religious concepts elicits a sustaining response from that hidden behavior of the universe which fulfills human life, then we will have a form of experimental verification. This, then, is his empirical method, in which ideas are derived from religious experience and tested in religious practice.

Wieman's description of religious experience is one of his better achievements and was one of the grounds for his being invited to the University of Chicago. He says that from the great mass of stimuli flowing over the organism at any moment, we select what is useful, interesting, or significant, ignoring the rest of the totality. This selection constitutes our "appreciable world," but since it is a selection, there is a great "waste of experience," a wider, deeper, richer range of experience we could come to appreciate. Wieman describes religious experience or "mysticism" as the immediate, non-discriminating awareness of, and openness to, the fullness of sensual experience which arises through the suspension of the valuing, selecting, and ordering functions of normal consciousness. This awaremess comes about, Wieman says, primarily due to bewilderment in crisis, when the system of habits is frustrated and attention becomes diffusive and unfocused; but it also arises through the influence of a love object, by intense encounter with others, through the effect of a crowd, in quiet introspection, or because of the experience of grandeur or beauty. Religious experience is "the state of diffusive awareness, where habitual systems of response are resolved into an undirected, unselective aliveness of the total organism to the total event then ensuing."[5] The datum of religious experience is this awareness of the total passage of nature, the undiscriminated total event. Religious experience is thus of a real object, and not simply of an imaginal construct, but it is not of a realm beyond nature or by means of a faculty separate from sense experience, as in the thought of James. Religious experience is a way of experiencing the natural world and is therefore continuous with other forms of experience.

Wieman relates his description of religious experience to the idea of the fulfillment of life. The effect of religious experience on the individual is that of rebirth and transformation, such that one is free from limiting patterns of perception and response, and one's appreciable world comes to include a more expansive selection from the total event. First, religious experience involves the breakdown of the habitual personality into a free play of impulse; the limitation on perception and response imposed by habitual patterns is momentarily suspended. Second, one undergoes the ecstatic experience of the richness of the total event out of which a more ample appreciable world can be made if new patterns of perception and response are developed. The free play of impulse may thus discover new patterns, which, if incorporated into the repertoire of the self, would yield a consciousness which is aware of a wider sector of the of the complex total event. A new outlook arises which is attentive to features of experience formerly overlooked, and if a conflict provoked the experience, the means of its resolution may now be perceived. Thus, new meanings or habits of perception and response arise in religious experience which expand the world we are able to experience. In addition, through religious experience the personality is unified, and conflicting impulses are more nearly fused into an integrated system. Finally, the one undergoing the experience has a renewed sense of the concrete fullness of the total event underlying our system of conscious meanings. In short, experience is enriched and made whole; it is this experience which, according to Wieman, creates the greatest good.

The Principle of Concretion

Wieman does not believe that the integration of the self and the expansion of its appreciable world is simply the result of the breakdown of habit and the experimental discovery of more fruitful patterns. Rather, there is an objective reason why the experience of the total event has an enriching and integrating effect. At work in the world itself there is a source of integration not usually perceived but effective in human life through religious experience. The self becomes more aware and a more integrated whole because religious experience involves the perception of the vast web of events as mutually sustaining and vivifying each other, as participating in an aesthetic order which is undergoing constant transformation.

The experience of the total event is the religious experience because it brings life again and again to greater completion; it does this because it is an intensification of one's experience of the divine order pervading the universe. It is the experience of God, in the sense that it is exposure to the unity and interrelatedness which constitutes the total event. It is the immediate, noncognitive awareness of the ultimate integration of all experience in one vast ordering process.

While the concept of the expansion and enrichment of our system of meanings or habits of perception and response is related to Dewey's thought, for Wieman as a religious realist it is not human effort or trial and error experimentation which unifies experience, but an objective, operative feature of nature. This concept of nature as embodying an active order is adapted from Whitehead.[6]

In Wieman's use of Whitehead's vision of an organic universe, each particular existent "prehends" all being, and all being is "concreted" in every existent; each object is just what it is because of the unique way it focuses the influence received from the rest of being. The concretion of a particular object is thus the unification of the many into one, and the way this occurs to form a particular object manifests the principle of concretion.

> To be concrete means precisely this entry of the many into the one. It involves this organization of being in such fashion that all participates in each and each in all. Nothing at all could be concrete if a wide realm of being were not so constituted as to come to a focus in each thing, thereby making it concrete. Now the principle of concretion is this structure of the universe by virtue of which all being does thus come to a focus in each thing.[7]

All being is concreted into the forms which actually exist because it is organized according to the principle of concretion, which is an active order which pervades it. This order which constitutes the concreteness of things is God.

> The character of all being that makes it a cosmos rather than a chaos is the principle of concretion. It is the principle which gathers up all being and packs it . . . into every grain of sand or flower or animal or person. It is that constitutive principle which gives concreteness to all being and hence gives actuality to the universe. It is that constitutive principle which rallies the whole universe to the making and sustaining of every concrete thing.[8]

The order which reflects the principle of concretion is not a conceptual or moral order, but an aesthetic order; that is, it is an order in which various diverse features work together to form a single effect.

Wieman had described the highest level of human life as one that interacts most intimately, extensively, and continuously with the total environment. It now can be seen that this life is attained if we are responsive to that order of being which operates to sustain and promote the growing integration of the universe. He suggests the term "universal love" for that ordering of all things in such a way that the whole enters most richly and fully into the existence of every particular. If God is this principle of concretion, then love is the fullest actualization of the divine order in a human life and the best adaptation to God.

Wieman's formal definition of God was that within the universe which fulfills human interests in the fullest, most harmonious way, rendering human life responsive to an ever wider and fuller environment. And he has proposed that what functions in this way is the principle of concretion. This principle brings about the progressive integration of the universe, increasing the responsiveness of every existent to the whole range of being. The highest good of human life is the human expression of the divine order, or the fulfillment of human interests when these interests are conformed to the order of the universe. In this way, the ideas of good as fulfilled interest and as prehension of the divine order are united.

The concept of God as the universe's progressive integration through the principle of concretion is offered as an objective concept of God, in that God is seen as an ordering of the universe, a certain character of concrete events, independent of human interests and knowledge. And (as Wieman interprets Whitehead) it is a naturalistic account of God, for the divine is within and not beyond the one world of events.

Yet it seems that there is a tension between the Deweyan empiricism of Wieman's method and the Whiteheadian speculative metaphysics which actually provides the concept of God in this phase of Wieman's thought. It may appear that the principle of concretion has been appropriated from Whitehead's system and grafted on to an essentially Deweyan structure; we are entitled to wonder if the principle of concretion proposed as the content of the concept of God in the second of these two early volumes is actually an inference from religious experience derived in the manner prescribed in the first volume, or whether it is instead simply an abstraction having a logically necessary place in Whitehead's metaphysics. But perhaps we should be more generous in interpreting Wieman. Religious experience as he describes it has a re-ordering effect on the personality such that it prehends being more richly, and this is the result of mysticism's openness to a creativity at work throughout the universe. Seen in that way, the use of Whitehead is a step in drawing inferences from religious experience.

Still, there is a problem. The principle of concretion does not seem to indicate the bare *fact that* the universe orders and reorders itself to increase the richness and variety of its concretions; rather, it seems to be an attempt to state *the reason why* the universe operates in this way. It is, in short, not an operational concept indicating the way things are, but an attempt at a metaphysical explanation. (This becomes clear when we recall that the principle of concretion is not manifest as a static order but as an active and endless re-ordering.) To the empiricist, the speculative metaphysician can be seen to be conceptualizing the observed behavior of the universe and then taking the resulting concept as an explanation of what is observed. This is like the antique explanation of the narcotic effect of opium: it causes sleep because of its "dormitive power." As Wieman was later to conclude, principles are not causes.

Wieman was brought to the University of Chicago partly because he could interpret the complex Whiteheadian cosmology. The great interest in Whitehead in the late 'twenties led Wieman to adapt for his own use the idea of the principle of concretion as that which operates through religious experience to expand human awareness. But the obvious tension between Wieman's empirical method and the principle of concretion taken as explanatory rather than as descriptive led him in the 'thirties, in ways which we have seen, to set aside the Whiteheadian idea and to attempt to speak of progressive integration or creative synthesis in strictly empirical terms. And then as Wieman's development led him increasingly to emphasize empirical method, the focus was to shift from the progressive integration of the universe to the progressive integration of the mind as a system of meanings through creative communication. We turn now to this third phase of his search for a naturalistic concept of the divine.

Value and Qualitative Meaning

The methodology of empiricism which is basic to Wieman's work had the effect of turning his interest from Whitehead's speculative metaphysics to the descriptive approach of his writings of the 'thirties, and then to a close examination of interpersonal communication as the matrix in which personality is transformed. This development culminated in Wieman's major work, *The Source of Human Good* (1946).

We can speak of three phases in Wieman's thought only because of our concentration on his search for a naturalistic concept of God; but as a matter of fact his thought shows great consistency throughout. The title of Wieman's major work expresses his formal definition of God as the source of human good. This definition and the concern for the empirical availability of the concept of God are continuities in his work. Wieman's motivation is the same in his later writings as in his earlier work, to formulate religious concepts usable by the current scientific mentality. Yet there is now a greater sense of urgency, and a more sophisticated use of empiricism. Here Wieman is not merely involved with the apologetics of liberal theology, but feels himself confronting an historical crisis. Because of the process of social change, traditional symbols are losing their power to guide commitment, and yet vastly increased technological power requires even more effective guidance than was provided by traditional ideas. A revival of traditional symbols is of no value, in his view, because they are not open to the use of rational-empirical method and thus cannot provide the needed guidance in the use of our magnified powers. "The desperate need of our time is for a faith that can direct our commitment to the creative source of all human good as it works in the temporal world, open to rational-empirical search and to service by modern technology."[9]

Wieman's naturalism is more fully stated in this phase. There is nothing in reality more accessible to mind than events, their qualities, and their relations; thus the divine must be seen as actually operative in the world of events. Wieman feels that in this approach he is affirming the spirit of biblical realism, in which the source of good is seen as working in history, as over against the Greek rational-speculative tradition, in which the good is seen as residing in a realm of timeless forms. Yet Wieman rejects the dualism present in both traditions, for God will be seen as the creative event itself, a creativity immanent in actual events in time and space, and not as the transcendent cause of experienced creativity.

If the divine is seen as that upon which the greatest good of human life depends, then, as in earlier phases of Wieman's work, religious inquiry must begin with a characterization of this good. The experienced datum for reflection is the immediate, inscrutable awareness of qualities as pertaining to complex events. Quality is ineffable and cannot be described or communicated; we can speak only of the conditions under which it is experienced. Knowledge of the conditions underlying experiences of quality provides "handles" for intellectual understanding and guidance of action. When we discover the connection between qualities and the events that are their conditions we have the power to alter the qualities in experience; this connection is "instrumental meaning."

"Qualitative meaning" is the relation between qualities, and is the means through which the good of human life increases. Qualitative meaning is that symbolic reference by which some events take on added significance by virtue of their reference to the qualities of other events. Some events come to be signs of other events, and through this process the richness of experience is increased, as wide realms of quality are focused in a single moment of experience.

> Qualitative meaning is that connection between events whereby present happenings enable me to feel not only the quality intrinsic to the events now occurring but also the qualities of many other events that are related to them. [It is] . . . that connection between events whereby the present happening conveys to me the qualities of other happenings and some qualities pertaining to what will happen in the future, as the future is interpreted by the past.[10]

Qualitative meaning is the symbolic reference which gathers together in one experience a rich mass of felt quality from myriad related events; the good of life increases when the richness of our experience grows through qualitative meaning.

This concept of the growth of good in human life is a more precise form of the concept in Wieman's earliest work of responsiveness to an ever wider and fuller environment.

The Creative Event

If God is that which increases the good of human life, then God is whatever is found to increase qualitative meaning. According to Wieman, there is an observable process at work in our midst that transforms the human mind and its appreciable world by weaving the web of meaning between events. The creative event is that which enriches experience and increases the good of human life by giving rise to qualitative meaning. This is a process of interpersonal communication and personal reorganization in which new meanings are conveyed and integrated with old, enriching one's system of meanings and endowing all events with a wider range of reference, "molding . . . life . . . into a more deeply unified totality of meaning."[11]

The creative event consists of four sub-events.

1. The emerging awareness of qualitative meaning derived from others through communication.

2. The integration of these new meanings with others previously acquired.

3. The expanding richness of quality in the appreciable world by the enlarging of meaning.

4. The deepening of community among those who participate in this total creative event of intercommunication.[12]

Notice that not all communication functions in this creative way; In some forms of communication we are evasive and do not disclose our own unique way of seeing things, and so the exchange is not creative; in other forms of communication we attempt to manipulate others, and they become closed to whatever insight we are attempting to communicate. Only a certain type of communication is creative, and Wieman's subsequent work included inquiry into the precise conditions which raise communication to the level of the creative event. In writings after *The Source of Human Good*, Wieman referred to this event as creative interchange, and it increasingly became his sole concern.

Creative interchange creates the mind as a system of meanings; and it creates the appreciable world, the world relative to the mind, although it does not create the physical world or the total event from which the appreciable world arises. The creative event is also the source of community between minds, as experience is shared and we come to include the thoughts and feelings of others in our system of meanings.

The influence of Dewey on Wieman is greater than that of Whitehead, although this is not generally recognized. In the concept of the creative event of intercommunication, Wieman has amplified and developed Dewey's notion of communication as the source of the system of meanings which is mind and culture. Concluding his analysis of the creative significance of communication, Dewey had written,

> When the emotional force, the mystic force one might say, of communication, of the miracle of shared life and shared experience is spontaneously felt, the hardness and crudeness of contemporary life will be bathed in the light that never was on land or sea.[13]

If we set aside what Dewey actually wrote about the term God (the topic of the next chapter) we might almost say that this is a naturalistic concept of the divine creativity, one that is very similar to Wieman's concept of creative interchange. It might be added that the distinction between the qualitative and instrumental character of events is also developed from Dewey.[14]

The result of creative interchange is a new structure of meanings whereby events are more widely and richly related in meaningful connection; this structure is created good, the appreciable world made richer through qualitative meaning, and is the substance of culture. But creative good is the process whereby such a structure comes about, and it is the object of religious commitment. Indeed, the greatest obstacle to creative transformation is our clinging to existing goods. Here we encounter again the creative-created distinction essential to theism and found in Wieman's writings of the 'thirties.

Both Wieman's theological realism and his naturalism are seen in his insistence that the creative event is not a human accomplishment, but neither is it the work of anything external to natural events; it is the result of a creativity which is a character of natural events, which transforms us as we cannot transform ourselves. Against the moralistic humanism of other naturalists such as Dewey, Wieman insists that human fulfillment depends not on good will, knowledge, and effort alone, but on adaptation to a superhuman power. Yet the creative event is not superhuman in the sense that it works outside of human life and nature, but in the sense that it does what we cannot do on the basis of the present order of our lives.

> To do what lies beyond the reach of . . . our imagination, a greater imagination must be created in us. To seek a good beyond what we

can appreciate, a greater appreciation must be developed in us. The creative event, and not ourselves, creates this greater imagination and this more profound and discriminating appreciation.[15]

Thus creative interchange functionally transcends humanity, but does not metaphysically transcend nature. It works beyond human effort but is not beyond the world of natural events, since it is precisely the creative character of certain events. According to Wieman, the idea of God in the older supernaturalism referred to this functional transcendence. The traditional symbol directed commitment to this immanent creativity, and associated rituals and practices prescribed the behavior which is adaptive to it, all without giving any actual knowledge of its character. In the concept of the creative event Wieman believed we possess knowledge of the divine creative activity.[16]

The concept of creative interchange is supposed to give us knowledge to replace failing myth and symbol. But Wieman preserves the biblical injunction against idolatry in his repeated insistence that religious commitment must be directed to that creativity actually operative in human life, and not to any particular concept of it, including his own. The Deweyan concept of the instrumental character of ideas leads Wieman to believe that true ideas relate us to events and processes in nature without disclosing their inner reality; thus the concept of the creative event is a tool useful in relating us to a creativity which it does not capture. The idea of creative interchange is a form of created good, but the object of religious devotion must be creative good.

Finally, while creative interchange does for us what the supernatural personal God was said to do, it is not a personal deity, but the creator of persons. Personality is a form of created good, but creative good is not itself a person.

So Wieman felt with some urgency that the breaking of the hold of traditional belief and practice on modern people made it necessary to be specific about the nature of the divine creativity operative in human life; creative interchange is the actual referent of the term God. He maintained that creative good is the absolute good, since it is good under all conditions. It provides a standard of value, in the sense that anything promoting or sustaining creative interchange is of value, and whatever either opposes or obstructs further creative transformation is evil, even if it is some form of created social good. Wieman felt that this fact provides a basis for a transcending of existing social values and thus for social criticism, and he contrasted this idea with the tendency of moralistic humanism simply to reflect already existing values.

But the creative event is not absolute in the sense that it is all-powerful. There is no guarantee that creativity will prevail in history, and while it cannot be destroyed by evil, it may well be reduced to working on levels more primary than the human. In this regard, Wieman observes that the creative event in human interchange does seem to parallel processes observed on the prehuman level of cosmic evolution. But his interest in exploring this dimension of the divine creative activity is much less in these writings of the 'forties and later than in his earlier studies.

The Rejection of Speculative Metaphysics

Wieman's empiricism and his sense of the loss of the power of inherited symbols and practices led him to insist that attention be focused on that creativity actually found to operate in human life. And increasingly, he claimed that speculation about this creativity being the manifestation of a metaphysically transcendent being or structure is misleading.

Wieman's objection to metaphysical speculation can be interpreted as having three strands, usually intertwined in his writing of this period. One is the simple, practical objection that giving attention to such questions directs our attention away from the world of experienced events, where alone we come to know and adjust to creative good. He insisted that concepts of the divine creative activity must guide decision-making in the present, and that visions of observed creativity as actually the effect of something more fundamental were useless in this regard.[17]

The second strand comes from empiricist philosophy in general and, more particularly, the pragmatism of James and Dewey. In this connection Wieman says that metaphysical abstractions are mere structures of possibility; they propose elements of thought supposed to be logically necessary to an intellectual grasp of being, but they are not testable objects of knowledge. The many metaphysical visions of ultimate reality are all alike compatible with the observed world; they are possible accounts of reality and whether one is true or false makes no difference in action.

The third strand of Wieman's thought which undermines confidence in metaphysical schemes seems like that of the Kantian critical philosophy, that visions of the structure of reality merely reflect the structure of the mind. Wieman states this outlook in his own way. The order we experience can be understood without reference to an alleged primordial structure of the world. Specifiable order arises through the selectivity of the senses of a particular organism, and symbol-using organisms can represent this order in thought. But organisms with different structures would experience a different order of nature. Therefore, we can have no knowledge of a primordial order beyond the order relative to our organic constitution and the present development of our consciousness. Claims about the primordial order of nature are simply structures of thought.

Wieman's argument against metaphysical beliefs unites these elements. From the total event of immediate experience, the noncognitive feeling reactions of the organism automatically select that which is specifiable for such an organism, thus constituting a world of events relative to that organism. In human life the specifiable structure defined by the feeling reactions of the organism then becomes specified in knowledge. The specified structure abstracted from the qualities of actual events is remote from concrete reality, and is useful merely as a guide to action; this is instrumental meaning, concepts useful in finding our way among the complexities of the world. The concept of creative interchange is just such a structure. It is a true concept of the divine creative activity, in that it accurately guides action into relation with creative good, but it is a concept and not a concrete reality experienced in feeling. Like all concepts, it is an abstract structure of possibility pertaining to events. Creative good itself must be seen as an actual character of events, rather than as any structure of abstraction. The concept of the supernatural first cause, or of Whitehead's principle of concretion, are likewise abstractions, and they are to be evaluated for their effectiveness as guides to action. Wieman feels that, contrasted with the idea of the creative event, these high-level abstractions fail as predictors of future experience.

For Wieman, truth is not all structures which might become specified, but those structures actually relevant to a particular level of
organic existence. Thus, there is no discoverable primordial order
of eternal objects or absolute ideas beyond the world of events as
appreciable to some organism. And that which gives rise to specified structure and the appreciable world is not a principle of concretion adjusting a world of forms to the passage of nature's process,
but the creative event operating in human life. The only kind of
structure not created by the creative event of communication is that
minimum structure which energy must have to be creative, and
which presumably operates on others levels of the universe.

In his early work, drawing from Whitehead, Wieman had said
that a particular world emerges from the undiscriminated wealth
of the total event through a primordial order prior to events. In this
last phase of his thought he now asserts that a particular world arises
in mind from this ground of all possible appreciable worlds through
the selectivity of an organism with certain sensory and symbol-using
capacities. In short, Wieman is aware that we understand reality
from within and not from above, as most metaphysicians claim to
do. A metaphysical system in this view merely describes in one possible way the structure necessary to thought; it does not describe
the one constitutive order of reality.

There is a determinate order of existence at any level of creation
which is the structure of the world constituted by the capacities of
a particular organism. There is a further determinate order running
through all levels of creation, which is the minimal structure necessary for energy to be creative of any order whatsoever. The first
order is relative to organic existence, and the second is not an abstract
order separate from and prior to events, but a character of events
themselves. (In the terminology I used before, it is the fact of order
and not the reason for it.) Knowledge is limited to these orders discoverable in the appreciable world and cannot extend beyond the
appreciable world of the organism to the supposed roots of this
world in a primordial order or a transcendent cause.[18]

It is now clear why Wieman rejects both traditional theistic and
modern process metaphysics, the visions of God as transcendent
first cause or principle of concretion. It should also be apparent why

he is less interested in the cosmic or non-human working of creativity than in the creativity of a certain sort of communication.

The Unity and Cosmic Dimension of God

If we contrast Wieman's early interest in the metaphysical concept of the principle of concretion with the concepts of God developed in his middle and later writings, God as creative synthesis and as creative interchange, a problem emerges. This is the problem of the unity of God.

As delineated by Wieman, the divine is a real, objective, experienceable, and operative character of events, but the actual elements of experience one might identify as ingredient in this creative occurrence are not the same in every occasion. To point to an actual manifestation of creative good in one instance is to indicate different elements than one would encounter in another. Various instances of the creative event have in common simply their character of being creative; this formal or functional likeness constitutes the only unity of the divine in Wieman's thought. This is true whether we are speaking of creative interchange acting in human life, or of creative synthesis as including this and also operating on other levels of existence. Metaphysical concepts like the principle of concretion seem to solve this problem, but for Wieman the solution is merely verbal.

If we contrast the later writings of Wieman, which center on the idea of creative interchange, with those of his earlier periods, a second problem emerges. This is the question of the cosmic dimension of the divine creative activity.

Religious devotion traditionally focuses on a cosmic God, a creativity at work on all levels of the cosmos and not just in human life. In his writings of the 'thirties he showed how creative good is at work on the level of non-living matter to produce a world and symbol-using organisms in the first place; then the creative event would simply be one of many manifestations of cosmic creativity on the human level. In his later thought emphasis is placed on the creative event which is limited to a certain kind of interchange between individuals characterized by candor, sympathy, receptiveness, and the absence of defensiveness and manipulation. It is the creative source of the appreciable world, but not of the non-human

universe and its evolving forms. Wieman grants that creative interchange is continuous with a larger creativity, but has little to say
about this. His declining interest in creativity as a universal process
may be the result of the growing influence of Dewey on Wieman's
thought, for Dewey limits philosophy to the description of the conditions of human experience and action. And it surely reflects
Wieman's sense that what modern people need is a highly specific
concept of creative good which can guide personal and social decisions. Wieman goes so far as to point out that this is the kind of
world in which the creative event can occur, and that energy must
have some minimal structure by virtue of which it is creative in order
to give rise to the evolving world and human life, but he insists that
we *cannot* have knowledge of the functioning of creativity beyond
human experience, and that we *should not* seek knowledge of its
operation outside creative interchange.

   If we see the unity and the cosmic activity of the divine as difficulties in Wieman's concept of God, it is well to note that both difficulties are created by his empiricist epistemology. Wieman came to
reject the Whiteheadian notion of the principle of concretion and
turned his interest away from creative synthesis as a universal
process, for the sake of the empirical availability of his concept of
God. Wieman might reply to the charge that his later work was
deficient in giving unity and universality to the divine simply by
accepting the problems as necessary if he is to construct a concept of
the divine which is a useful guide to action. The seeming unity provided by the more speculative approach of his earliest work seems
to him to be merely verbal, and the interest in the cosmic working of
creativity appears to him in his later years as a distraction.

Chapter Four

Humanism

Within the kind of naturalistic thought we are examining, the object of religious commitment must be nature as a whole or its dominant feature, the ideal of human welfare as a focus of social action, or a creative ground of human good immanent within nature which is more than human effort. In short, the forms of religious philosophy available within naturalism are pantheism, humanism, or naturalistic theism. Wieman is significant for his interest in this rarely explored third option. The rejection of the humanistic choice among his colleagues at Chicago was made in discussions during the 'twenties, and the outcome of this was examined in the first chapter. But a famous debate between Wieman and John Dewey and others, in the pages of the journal *Christian Century* in 1934–1935, made clear just what is involved in the choice between religious humanism and naturalistic theism. We now turn to an examination of this exchange.

The debate was occasioned by the publication of Dewey's book *A Common Faith* (1934), which is supposed to have elicited from George Santayana the comment "all too common." Wieman's vigorous response to this book can now be seen to be based on a misunderstanding of Dewey, and as we explore the basis for this misunderstanding we will discover the important difference between the American naturalism basic to Wieman's reflection and that mechanistic and reductionistic materialism which is also sometimes called naturalism.

Critical Naturalism

When Dewey turned somewhat late in his career to the task of interpreting religious life and thought, Wieman and other religious naturalists were predisposed to expect him to develop a form of

naturalistic theism rather than the religious humanism which he did
in fact present. They did this because of the tendency of Dewey's
critical naturalism to stress the continuity of human life with the
natural forces on which it depends.

The stalemate of idealism and materialism in nineteenth-century
thought was the problem which generated critical naturalism.
Materialism took as its primary fact the physical sciences, and it
developed a picture of the world as a system of force and matter.
Consequently, the complexities of the human world could be
reduced through analysis to factors which are themselves devoid of
value, purpose, or meaning. If the fundamental reality were dead,
valueless matter moving in accidental, pointless patterns, then it
seemed that there was no place for the uniquely human concerns
for ethical choice, artistic creation, and the vision of the world as
meaningful. The uniquely human activities of choosing, valuing,
creating, and hoping could be explained through the activities of
more fundamental realities understood through biology and chem-
istry. Human life was seen as an accidental by-product of impersonal forces, irrelevant to an understanding of reality as it is.

Reacting against this scientifically plausible but humanly unsat-
isfying view, idealism took as its primary fact human life itself.
Idealism was a defense of the uniquely human experiences of subjective interiority, moral choice, artistic creativity, and religious
insight against the claim that they are ephemeral and not genuine
disclosures of reality. Idealism's world was not a system of force and
matter but the expression of will and thought. Fundamental reality was seen as cosmic mind, and the world, its thoughts. Just as
materialism reduced the uniquely human to material particles, so
idealists reduced the world of natural science to mere appearance,
as contrasted with the ultimate reality of mind. Here human life was
at home in a congenial world, and now it was science that was
regarded as irrelevant to an understanding of reality.

Philosophical interpretation was divided, therefore, between an
anti-scientific and reactive celebration of human cultural creativity,
and a scientific mechanism which lacked the ability to understand
the uniquely human on its own terms.

This impasse between materialism and idealism in the nineteenth
century can be seen as the failure to understand the place of human

life in nature. It seemed to the American naturalists that materialism described matter while ignoring its power to create life and
thought; therefore, it misunderstood matter. But idealism appeared
to them to be equally one-sided. It developed an appreciative view
of the ideal creations of mind but it failed to see their basis in material conditions; therefore it misunderstood mind. The naturalists
chose the term "nature" to indicate that inclusive whole which is
disclosed in both physical science and human cultural creativity.

George Santayana was the first to develop a critical or non-
reductive naturalism which would combine an acceptance of scientific method and its results with an appreciative interpretation of
human culture. This was to be the "new naturalism."

In the five volumes of *The Life of Reason* (1905–1906) Santayana
set about to give an account of human culture as the development
of our organic impulses operating within the natural world; his project was "the naturalizing of the imagination."[1] He portrayed mind
as the epiphenomenal product of natural forces, related to them as
the foam to the waves. Mind is a product of nature, but it merely
reflects and evaluates the passage of nature and does not operate as
a participant intervening in the flow of events. It is an incidental
product of nature which bestows value on an otherwise meaningless machine. Human ideals are imaginative projections of the fulfillment sought by animal impulses, visions of the satisfaction
implied in interests; they function as standards of valuation by which
natural events are judged and given meaning. However, the actual
satisfaction of interests depends solely on the operation of natural
causes. While we should have "piety" toward the natural process
on which life depends, the higher element in religion is "spirituality" which is the contemplative ordering of conscious life according to the vision of the ideal. Indeed, the divine element in experience
is the human ideal; God is "the ideal synthesis of all that is good,"[2]
the comprehensive vision of life as it ought to be, by which life as it
is is ordered and given value. This conception of the divine amounts
to a somewhat Platonic religious humanism.

Most of those committed to the new critical naturalism concluded
that Santayana was its Moses, in that he saw the promised land but
did not enter it.[3] It is true that he accepted the vision implied in the
science of his day and that this served as the causal background for

a sensitive and non-reductive account of the uniquely human; but spirit and nature remain for Santayana two distinct realms, one the order of causes and the other the source of value. His older colleague at Harvard, Josiah Royce, characterized his intent as the systematic separation of essence and existence.[4] He seems to have accepted both the mechanist's vision of the world as a meaningless machine and the idealist's desire to isolate imaginal products from contamination by the material. Thus, there is a lingering dualism in his philosophy.

It came to be accepted that the fulfillment of the project of critical naturalism must stress to a greater degree the continuity of the human and the non-human. Many felt that this goal was best embodied in the thought of John Dewey of Columbia University, especially in his Carus Lectures published as *Experience and Nature* (1925, revised 1929).

The root metaphor of much of Dewey's thought is the biological image of the organism interacting with the environment; this, in turn, generates the concept of the event as a basic category in Dewey's naturalistic metaphysics. In the event of interaction there are two poles, the human and the non- human, and the emergent character of the event as a whole is the result of the interpenetration of these two. We notice that every interactive event has a qualitative aspect as well as causal relations with other events. Dualistic thinking normally says that this qualitative character is contributed by the sensitive organism; but just as it would be an error to say that qualities are simply in objects themselves, so it is a mistake to say that they reside solely in our reactions; they are neither merely subjective nor objective, but contextual, characters of the total context of interaction of subject and object. Experiences of quality therefore reveal genuine traits of nature; that is, qualities are traits which objects come to have in interactions with sensitive organisms.

Dewey contrasts his approach with the "fallacy of intellectualism," his term for the tendency to select one aspect of complex events and to explain the whole through this part, which alone is regarded as "real." Here a selection made for some purpose is transformed into a definition of reality, whereas the real is in fact the complex whole itself. Both idealism and materialism commit this fallacy, but in contrasting ways. Materialism selects for attention the causal connections between events, because it is by virtue of these that one event may serve as an instrument for influencing another. This aspect then is taken as "the real," and the qualitative richness of events is reduced to "mere appearance," a subjective imposition on events. But the qualities of events are, according to Dewey, just as natural as their mechanistic connections. Thus aesthetic and moral experience reveal nature just as surely as does our rational-instrumental experience. Ignoring the qualitative aspect of events, and treating their instrumental aspect as alone real, yields the distorted view of nature as dead mechanism.

Note that this is a criticism both of nineteenth-century materialism, that is, the old naturalism, and of Santayana's attempt at a new naturalism. A further difference between Santayana and Dewey lies in their interpretations of the ideal. Human ideals are for Dewey imaginative visions of possible perfectings of natural tendencies; they are like the anticipation of the eighth note when nature has sounded the first seven of an octave. When once imagined, the ideal then functions as a guide to action, in which humans intervene in the flow of events to reconstruct experience. As to their origin, ideals are not just projections of desire but also the discovery of natural possibilities relevant to them; they are not subjective but contextual. And as to their function, they are not objects of contemplation but plans of action. In the process of the reconstruction of experience guided by the ideal, human and non-human factors interact, nature suggesting the possible perfecting of its tendencies and providing forces and materials, and the human community providing the vision of possibilities and the coordination of nature's resources.

To grasp what Wieman expected to find in Dewey's treatment of religion, we must understand the contrast between Santayana and Dewey, and this can be clarified further by a glance at Santayana's review of *Experience and Nature* and Dewey's reply, both published in the *Journal of Philosophy*.

Santayana understood naturalism as the primacy of the order of causes. Therefore, he saw *Experience and Nature* as a reduction of nature to the terms of human experience, a retreat from naturalism to idealism. Against this, Santayana claimed that we must see nature itself as the great background of human life, and not as it appears from the perspective of the human foreground. When we adopt some privileged perspective from which to view things, we have metaphysics, and this will be of different sorts depending on what occupies the foreground, whether logic, moral striving, or religious insight. To Santayana, Dewey's "naturalistic metaphysics" is just the latest way of making the human foreground dominant. "His naturalism is half-hearted and short-winded. It is a specious kind of naturalism."[5] The result is, according to Santayana, that nature is seen as having the values which it only receives through human acts of valuation. However, when nature is humanized through the dominance of the foreground, it is misunderstood. Values are not revelations of nature, but of human interests. Only that view is naturalistic which sees nature without adopting a privileged perspective.

Dewey replied that Santayana's view was "broken-backed naturalism." According to Dewey, Santayana fails to see human experience as a disclosure of nature; that is, he has failed to see the human foreground as the foreground *of nature*. His naturalism is "broken-backed" because it is "the structural dislocation of non-human and human existence."[6] Dewey grants that there is no privileged perspective for interpreting nature and that human life is merely one perspective; he merely wants to claim that every perspective reveals some potential of nature.

To summarize, Santayana seems to claim that human life cannot be understood apart from its rooting in nature, but somehow nature is to be understood apart from its power to produce human life and values. Dewey believes that we have not understood nature if we ignore its manifest capacity to generate human life and culture. If we portray nature without reference to its potential to produce acts of valuing in human life, we must see it as valueless and meaningless. Dewey accuses Santayana of the intellectualist fallacy in that he has given attention to the instrumental relations of events in characterizing nature, and has depicted their qualitative aspect as unnatural and humanly imposed. It is true that Santayana is not a reductionist, for he does not deny the reality of the excluded aspect; but he is a dualist because he does not see this aspect as a genuine disclosure of nature's character.

Santayana had identified the divine with one aspect of his dualism of spirit and nature; the divine is the human ideal, a projected vision of the fulfillment of human life. This is a humanism in the style of Ludwig Feuerbach. We might expect Dewey as the critic of

Santayana's lingering dualism to propose a different interpretation of the divine. Would not a naturalistic theism be possible on the basis of Dewey's emphasis on the continuity of the human and the non-human? For Dewey has said that through the interaction of the human and the non-human the ideal arises as a vision of possibilities latent in natural conditions; and it is through the interaction of non-human materials and intelligent effort that there is the growth of good. The divine might then be defined within this sort of naturalism as that interaction in which life moves toward fulfillment. This might even seem more characteristic of Dewey than an emphasis on the human element alone. Since this interaction includes but also transcends human effort, to identify it as the divine element in nature, the source of life's fulfillment, would be a naturalistic theism. This possible interpretation of Dewey's naturalism was in fact anticipated by Wieman in an article in the *Journal of Religion* before Dewey's *A Common Faith* was published.[7]

Dewey's Religious Humanism

If the previous section establishes the *basis* of Wieman's misunderstanding of Dewey, the *object* of his misunderstanding was Dewey's study of religion found in his Terry Lectures delivered at Yale University in 1934 and published later that year as *A Common Faith*. Dewey's announced purpose was to emancipate the unifying and motivating power of religious life from dependence on beliefs about the supernatural. He defined the religious experience as the unification of the self and the concomitant harmonizing of life with its natural context. This actually occurs, he maintained, through our being conquered and claimed by the authority of the ideal, through our devotion to a comprehensive vision of the good. The religious experience is thus "the unification of the self through allegiance to inclusive ideal ends."[8] God is for Dewey the symbol for this inclusive ideal; God simply means "the unity of all ideal ends arousing us to desire and action."[9]

This view of the divine clearly is derived from Santayana's thought. Indeed, even though the naturalists rejected Santayana's attempt to work out a new naturalism, again and again when they came to religion they simply repeat his view rather than make a fresh analysis. However, in the above formulation of the concept of the divine, we must recall that for Dewey the ideal is not merely the human dream of a life which would satisfy impulse, but the vision of the completion of tendencies in nature which are relevant to life's fulfillment. In forming the ideal, we do not impose our imaginings on a valueless world but discover possibilities of transformation which inhere in natural conditions when they are viewed from the human perspective.

Therefore, Dewey expands his definition of the divine to make clear its relation to non-human factors.

> This idea of God, or of the divine, is . . . connected with all the natural forces and conditions—including . . . human association—that promote the growth of the ideal and that further its realization. We are in the presence neither of ideals completely embodied in existence nor yet of ideals that are mere rootless . . . fantasies, utopias. For there are forces in nature and society that generate and support the ideals. They are further unified by the action that gives them coherence and solidarity. It is this *active* relation between ideal and actual to which I would give the name "God."[10]

> Whether one gives the name "God" to this union, operative in thought and action, is a matter of individual decision. But the function of such a working union of the ideal and actual seems to me to be identical with that force that has in fact been attached to the conception of God in all the religions that have a spiritual content; and a clear idea of that function seems to me to be urgently needed at the present.[11]

Thus, Dewey's amplified conception of the divine is as the active relation of ideal and actual. The divine is the symbol for the ideal understood in its natural context, "a clear and intense conception of the union of ideal ends with actual conditions."[12] This contextualist view contrasts with Santayana's view of the divine as the ideal alone. Yet the activity which relates ideal and actual is, after all, human vision and effort. Dewey understands that there are two poles in the interaction in which visions of the good arise and grow toward fulfillment, but it is clear that for him the creative, coordinating role is played by intelligent action. The divine is the active relating of ideal and actual which occurs through human thought and work.

Dewey criticizes supernatural theism because it claims that the ideal is realized already in a realm beyond nature. He felt that this made the concept of the divine dependent on a dubious metaphysics and therefore rendered it powerless for an increasing number of people. In addition, he felt that for believers it represents wishful thinking which undermines enthusiasm for efforts to improve actual conditions in this world. But he was also critical of a certain type of Promethean humanism which divorced ideal and actual, and portrayed nature as indifferent or even hostile to human ends. "The essentially un-religious attitude is that which attributes human achievement and purpose to humanity in isolation from the world of physical nature. . . . Our successes are dependent upon the cooperation of nature."[13] Dewey chose to use the term God in order to suggest the relevance of nature's powers and potentialities to the growth of human good, and to inculcate that humility and trust which are necessary to a knowledge of and adjustment to natural conditions.

Of course for Dewey, the divine does not refer to nature as a whole but aspects selected by their relevance to human good. The concept of the divine

> . . . selects those factors in existence that generate and support our idea of good as an end to be striven for. It excludes a multitude of forces that at any given time are irrelevant to this function. Nature produces whatever gives reinforcement and direction but also what occasions discord and confusion. The "divine" is thus a term of human choice and aspiration.[14]

For Dewey, the divine symbolizes the cooperation of human and non-human forces in the growth of human good; it includes the dependence of the sought-for fulfillment on natural conditions and the creative role of intelligent human effort. Thus Dewey's interpretation of the divine element in human experience integrates Santayana's ideas of piety and spirituality into one rational-emotive movement, whereas in Santayana the two look in different directions. For Santayana, piety is directed toward our roots in nature, and spirituality is the contemplation of the human ideal; but for Dewey both have a single object, the divine as the coordination of ideal and actual in human striving. Nevertheless, Dewey is a religious humanist and not a naturalistic theist; while the interaction of human and non-human in the fulfillment of life is clearly stated, the emphasis is on the unifying role of human action.

As will be seen, religiously interested naturalists seemed to feel that it was more consistent with the naturalistic vision to insist on the dependence of the human active, organizing contribution itself upon the total natural context in which it occurs. This would constitute a naturalistic theism.

The Christian Century Discussion

In November of 1934, there appeared in *Christian Century* a review of Dewey's *A Common Faith* written by Wieman which interpreted Dewey as a naturalistic theist. In December of that year, *Christian Century* carried a criticism of Wieman's interpretation by his colleague at the University of Chicago E.E. Aubrey, and a note from Dewey confirming Aubrey's interpretation of the book. In the same issue Wieman replied to both Aubrey and Dewey; he abandoned the position that Dewey *intended* a theistic view but maintained that such a view was a warranted conclusion on the basis of his philosophic vision as a whole. Later in December the editor of the journal, Charles Clayton Morrison, reviewed the discussion between Wieman, Aubrey, and Dewey and suggested that Wieman in fact had developed implications in Dewey's philosophy which were not obvious to Dewey himself. A letter from Wieman's colleague Charles Hartshorne was printed in a subsequent issue stating that, while Wieman's interpretation of Dewey might have been in error, the thesis that Dewey's thought can be used in the development of a naturalistic theism is sound. In early January Dewey declined the editor's invitation to respond. A closer analysis of this interesting exchange will show that Wieman's misunderstanding of Dewey was revealing and significant.

Wieman's review of *A Common Faith* emphasized Dewey's recognition of the forces in nature and society which lie beyond and beneath human intelligence and imagination, to the extent that Dewey's actual intention of stressing the creative and active role of human thought and action is obscured. Wieman at first did not perceive Dewey's intention of stressing the creativity of the human pole in the interaction which gives rise to the ideal. Thus, according to Wieman, Dewey has defined the activity which unites ideal and actual as the interaction of human effort with natural conditions, and not merely as conscious, intelligent effort. In this interaction, the controlling power is not the human aim but the interaction itself, for human purposes are deflected and reshaped in their interaction with conditions.

According to Wieman's interpretation of Dewey, insofar as this interaction is the source of the growth of the good, it is the rightful object of supreme devotion, the naturalistic equivalent of God. The process which connects ideal and actual is not, of course, supernatural, but it is superhuman, in the sense that it is more than human intelligence and action. It is not superhuman in the sense that it can operate wholly apart from human life, or that it is itself intelligent and purposive; but it does transcend human imagination, since it is this interaction which creates human personality and its ideals, and which generates possibilities of value beyond those which human imagination can envision apart from this interaction. The generation and realization of ideal ends is dependent on our submitting ourselves to this supreme good, to receive that which it can bestow. Thus, Wieman's interpretation of Dewey stresses the total context of the interaction of human imagination and natural conditions in the growth of human welfare. He considers Dewey a naturalistic theist rather than a humanist.[15] The question of whether this interpretation is an improvement on Dewey's actual position remains for later consideration; at this point it is sufficient to say that insofar as Wieman felt that this view was Dewey's actual belief, Wieman was in error.

In reply to Wieman, Aubrey pointed out that such a position is not present in *A Common Faith*. He suggested that Wieman had read into Dewey's book his own opinion. The phrase "forces in nature and society which generate and support ideals" is interpreted by Wieman as meaning the "more than human principle of progressive integration operative in the cosmos and partly in humanity," according to Aubrey. However, for Dewey the phrase is taken "as affirming the power of corporate human intelligence to draw the actual given of nature and the projected ideals of the human imagination together in a plan of directed activity."[16] Human intelligence is, according to Dewey, the integrative power relating actual and ideal. Dewey wishes to point to the creativity of human intelligence, and while he allows for the role of natural conditions in the growth of good, it is not these conditions that are creative. Aubrey concludes that no counterpart of the transhuman process of progressive integration in Wieman's thought can be found in the Terry Lectures.

Wieman's response to Aubrey continued the emphasis on the total context of thought and action. According to Wieman, Dewey implies that there are activities going on in nature which *include* intelligent human effort, but which are more than this effort. These activities constitute the matrix in which intelligence develops. It is this matrix which gives rise to mind and ideals, and with which intelligent effort seeks to harmonize itself. Thus, there is an operative system of inter-functioning activities which at best includes human thought and effort as an ingredient, and it is this community of interaction which includes but goes beyond human intelligence, and which unites actual and ideal.[17]

Dewey's contribution to the exchange settled the question of the interpretation of *A Common Faith* but it may not have settled the broader question of whether human action or the total context in which it functions is appropriately assigned the creative role in a naturalistic religious philosophy. Dewey pointed out that it was his intention in *A Common Faith* to state that the term God might be applied to the role of human imagination in grasping the "union of ideals ... with some natural forces that generate and sustain them."[18] The unification of the various forces and conditions which generate and sustain our ideals is the work of human imagination and will. The efficacy of natural conditions depends upon the work of intelligence in discovering them and adjusting to them. The matrix in which ideals arise is the life of the human community, not non-human nature. Nature supports evil as well as good, and the selection of those forces fostering good is the work of human thought and will.

Wieman then admitted his error in interpreting *A Common Faith*, but continued to argue as to whether that which unites actual and ideal is human creativity, or a transhuman process which includes it and extends beyond it.

According to Wieman, human imagination is only one of many activities which make possibilities of value realizable. Before human intelligence existed, its emergence was a possibility of value in the then existent world, and its emergence is the result of the action of processes beyond it.

> Possibilities of value are rooted and grounded ... in a system of activities which interact in such a way as to make these possibilities practicable goals of endeavor when humans discover them. So likewise, human choice and action are activities shaped and sustained by many other activities which reciprocally shape and sustain them in a total system of interacting activities.[19]

This is a clear statement of Wieman's naturalistic theism and of his concept of creative synthesis as it had developed in the early 'thirties, but using the terminology of Dewey.

Wieman states that it would be consistent with Dewey's view to affirm this, and that it is the position one would expect to find in the light of the passages in which Dewey speaks of the natural basis of ideal projections and the dependence of human life on natural conditions. Dewey clearly denies that human activities stand in isolation from nature; thus, Wieman expects that he should affirm that human activities are part of a community of processes which so interact as to unite the actual and the ideal.

Dewey had said that selection and coordination of the manifold natural factors which generate and sustain ideals is the creative task of intelligence. Apart from this imaginative unification, the natural conditions relevant to human ideals are a mere collection of unrelated items. Thus, that which actually gives rise to idealizations of nature and coordinates the factors relevant to their realization is human thought. Dewey had in fact stated this argument prior to the *Christian Century* exchange.[20] Dewey's humanistic intent had also been manifest in his signing of the "Humanist Manifesto" in the winter of 1932–1933.[21] Against this argument, Wieman states that there is an inherent unity in these conditions whereby they interact to make ideals discoverable and realizable; the manifold natural conditions relevant to ideals are unitary with respect to their performance of one function. They will cooperate to perform this function apart from any human knowledge of their operation. "All activities that interact in such a way as to carry the highest possibilities of value, constitute a unitary system of interaction with respect to this one function of generating and sustaining these highest possibilities."[22]

Wieman asserts that when we imagine ideal possibilities in unity with their natural conditions, we create neither these possibilities nor the relevance of natural conditions to their growth. Thus, human efforts are among the processes which work together in the growth of good; and they, together with all other processes which serve this one function, constitute a unity which has the value of the divine. It is the functioning together for possibilities of human fulfillment which makes these activities a unity. They are one in their effect, and when this unity is made explicit in human thought it is a discovery and not a creation. Against Dewey's emphasis on the creative role of human effort, Wieman is asserting that even this contribution must be seen as part of a larger matrix of natural factors upon which it is dependent.

In reviewing the course of this exchange between Dewey and Wieman, the editor of the journal observed that Dewey made all of the affirmations necessary to Wieman's thesis in his book and in his reply to Wieman's review. That is, quite apart from Dewey's humanistic intention, a naturalistic theism is *possible* within the terms of Dewey's analysis of religion. In a letter, Charles Hartshorne made essentially the same point. Wieman's initial interpretation of *A Common Faith* was in error, according to Hartshorne, but the thesis that Dewey's philosophy provides a basis for a naturalistic theism is sound.[23]

Wieman's Misunderstanding of Dewey

Dewey's intention in *A Common Faith* was to say that while conditions make ideal ends possible, human efforts, through their unifying, integrating, coordinating function, make them actual. He wished to include the idea that human efforts work upon pre-existing materials merely in order to remind us that we can expect a supportive response to our efforts only if our goals and our means are intelligently conceived, and thereby take account of the context of action.

Yet it is possible within naturalism to identify the creative factor in the growth of human good with the total situation of interaction. Indeed, such a naturalistic theism which identifies the divine with the superhuman but not supernatural creativity upon which the good of human life depends, might be more consistent with Dewey's picture of human life as embedded in nature.

Perhaps the reason for Dewey's choice in emphasizing the human pole of the interaction which leads to the growth of good is his energetic participation in the optimistic progressivism of his day; his humanism seem to reflect the interest in social reconstruction and the impatience with tradition which characterized the liberal reformers of that time. This attitude stands in contrast with Wieman's openness to gifts from a source that undergirds human effort and transforms human ideals. This point makes clear that what is at stake on the human level in this choice of emphasis is different self-understandings; humanism and theism are antithetical under-standings of the human condition.

A few years after the *Christian Century* discussion, Charles Hartshorne suggested that Dewey's most important contribution to the reconstruction of religious ideas may not lie in his avowed humanism, but in his inadvertent suggestion of the possibility of a naturalistic theism.

> Great men, it seems, do modify the course of history, but it is well said that they seldom do so in just the direction they intend. Professor Dewey has sought to lead us from supernaturalism to a not too egregiously atheistic naturalism. It is possible that, somewhat indirectly at least, he may prove a principle creator of what may appear as the twentieth cen-tury's supreme theoretical discovery—theistic naturalism.[24]

Thus, Wieman's misunderstanding reveals that Dewey uninten-tionally provides materials for a naturalistic theism; and so it is an instructive misunderstanding, one which elucidates that which is misunderstood.[25]

Chapter Five

Pantheism

As we have seen, the American naturalists maintained that within the world of observable events the object of religious devotion might be identified with the dominant power shaping nature as a whole, human ideals and the effort to direct life toward their embodiment, or an immanent and finite creativity upon which the good of human life depends. Wieman argued against the first two options, pantheism and religious humanism, in two famous debates, one with John Dewey in 1934, discussed in the previous chapter, and the second with William Bernhardt in the *Journal of Religion* (1943–44).

The Journal of Religion Discussion:
Is God Dominant Power or Source of Value?

Bernhardt had been Wieman's student at the University of Chicago. In March of 1942 he wrote an essay in *Religion in the Making* which I maintain was designed to make clear the difference between his teacher's naturalistic theism and the pantheistic direction of his own thought, although these terms are not used. He claimed that the reconstruction of the concept of God within religious naturalism must begin with a decision about what kind of reality the divine is; specifically, is the divine to be understood as the dominant power in nature, or as the source of human good? Wieman initiated correspondence with Bernhardt, replying that the first question for inquiry about the divine was rather that of immanence and transcendence; he added, in response to Bernhardt's claim, that the quest for a naturalistic concept of God should seek for the source of human good. As a naturalist Bernhardt agreed on the absolute immanence of the divine, but he claimed that Wieman had never defended his choice of value over power in framing a concept of God. It seems that Bernhardt is correct in this observation. As the correspondence developed, Bernhardt introduced a third topic by asking, if the divine is the source of good operative in the observable world as Wieman claims, why is not perceived? Thus, the correspondence included three questions: is the divine to be understood through its value or its power? is it immanent within or transcendent over nature? and is the divine perceived or inferred? The correspondence led to the publication of four essays and a letter in the *Journal of Religion*.

This chapter will examine the published materials and will deal only with the first issue regarding power and value. We will see that what is actually at stake in the discussion is the choice between naturalistic theism and pantheism: within religious naturalism, should the divine be conceived as the dominant power that governs nature or as a creativity within nature that makes for human good?[1]

In the essay which provoked the correspondence between the two naturalists,[2] Bernhardt claimed that the first issue for those seeking to refashion the concept of deity was the question of the category for God: how is the divine to be classified, what sort of reality is it? I imagine humanists like Dewey would say that it is a concept of the most inclusive ideal. Bernhardt and Wieman have rejected this approach; they are theological realists, conceiving of God as a reality operating within the natural world.

Bernhardt suggests two sorts of realism, "agathonic realism" and "pure realism." The first he calls a "moral-personal approach;" it conducts religious inquiry on the basis of a categorization of the divine as the source of human good. The second view, his own, is said to be scientific and objective; inquiry is to seek that which is the dominant or controlling factor in existence, whether this is valuable for humans or not.

According to Bernhardt, the basis for the choice between power and value as the category to which deity belongs is our conception of the function of religion; if its function is the fulfillment of human life we will choose the category of value, and if it is the reconciliation of humans to aspects of life beyond their control, we will choose the dynamic category.

These claims provoked the correspondence between Wieman and Bernhardt. In the first of the published essays which summarized the correspondence,[3] Wieman acknowledged the issue but did not defend his choice; instead he discussed the problem of the perception of the divine, defined as the source of value. He claimed that the reason we do not perceive the divine creative activity is that we have no concepts to guide us into relation with it. Supernatural beliefs did not indicate an observable creativity (although Wieman believes that it was a creativity immanent within nature that was the actual power experienced in traditional religion), and the contemporary attempt to develop an operational concept of nature's creativity is only beginning.

Against Bernhardt's claim that God is that which exercises supreme control over the course of events and human life, Wieman asserts that the category for God must be goodness or value. He states that he and Bernhardt agree that because of the fact of evil in the world, the greatest good and the controlling power cannot be the same entity or process. Wieman grants that the greatest good may have some power and that the dominant power may show some supportiveness for human good; but the question is which concept will guide naturalistic inquiry. Thus he recognizes the issue raised by Bernhardt but postpones discussing it until a later essay.

William Bernhardt: the Divine as Dynamic Determinant

The case for construing the divine in naturalistic terms beginning with the category of power is made by Bernhardt in two essays in the series.[4] I claim it amounts to an argument for pantheism as the appropriate direction of development of American religious naturalism.

Every God-concept stresses either value or power, or as Bernhardt preferred to express it, the agathonic or the dynamic. He felt that the choice of classification of the divine as agathonic or dynamic was the first question for naturalistic religious inquiry. The reason for this position is that only when we know what kind of reality is the subject of investigation can we collect and analyze data; thus, the category in which we place the divine is a "data- and method-determinant." Subsequent analysis will yield a God-concept; in Bernhardt's terms, concepts are "data-explicants."

If we choose the agathonic category we do not necessarily deny power to God completely; Bernhardt recognizes that Wieman's naturalistic theism is a concept of God as the power that creates human good but is not the dominant power in nature. Similarly, if we choose the dynamic category, then we believe that value depends on power; that is, we give maximum value and devotion to the power that dominates nature. Although Bernhardt never uses the term, this seems clearly to be pantheism.

Bernhardt criticizes his teacher for failing to outline a method which would lead to a justification of the choice of the selective criterion of human value. Bernhardt's own method is this: first we are to establish the function of religion, and then deduce from this the category for deity.[5]

The function of religion is to deal with the non-manipulable aspects of life so as to sustain serenity. This function is performed at first through meta-technological or magical techniques which attempt to direct divine powers against threats and uncertainties. And it is accomplished, subsequently, through reinterpretations of the situation, such that emotion is redirected and impossibility accepted.

> Religion is a complex form of individual and group behavior whereby persons are prepared intellectually and emotionally to meet the unsatisfactory and inescapable aspects of existence positively, i.e., with confidence, courage, and hope.[6]

As knowledge and skill increase, situations which were formerly uncertain and precarious become more settled. For ancients, perhaps much ritual magic was involved in food production, even though they made use of a measure of simple technology; in the modern economy of abundance there is virtually no ritual involved in food-production. This implies a shift from a view of nature as lacking power and as dependent on the supernatural, to a view of nature as containing within itself the power to produce the values it includes. Finally, if through the increase of knowledge our view of nature is rich enough to serve as the explanation of all it contains, God-as-supernatural vanishes completely. In my interpretation of Bernhardt, this claim means that nature comes to function as the divine.

Developing his theory of the function of religion, Bernhardt observes that magical techniques are not effective, and as technology advances, the meta-technology of ritual declines in prominence in religion. The reason that religion survives despite this decline is that it has other benefits; it is capable of nurturing emotional composure through the reinterpretation of problematic situations. Thus, religion comes increasingly to center on spiritual change rather than on the manipulation of objective conditions.

The example Bernhardt gives of the shift from magical techniques to reinterpretation and spiritual change is a passage in the letters of Paul (II Corinthians 12.7–10). Here Paul says he prayed that God would remove a source of torment he calls his "thorn in the flesh," but when this did not occur it is evident that he came to interpret this difficulty as an opportunity to share in the suffering of Christ. "Whereas men have often besought God to change external conditions to suit their needs, they have always recognized the possibility that the change would have to be made in their own souls."[7] The progress of religion, for Bernhardt, is the increase of this aspect of religion, and the decline and disappearance of magical ritual and prayer. It seems to me that the final development would be a religion which teaches acceptance of whatever the power of nature bestows upon us, which is the ethos of pantheism.

The second step in Bernhardt's method is to deduce the category for deity from this analysis of the function of religion. In early phases of religion, the gods are seen as the power that governs nature and human life, and magic seeks to appropriate this power. As religion advances, this attempt to intervene in the course of nature through magic declines, and emphasis shifts to the gaining of inner poise through acceptance of whatever divine power bestows. And as noted above, this change coincides with the shift from God-as-supernatural to the locating of divine power within nature. Throughout the growth of religion, in both the magical and more spiritual phases, God is seen, in the phrase of J.B. Pratt, as "the determiner of destiny," or in Bernhardt's term, as "dynamic determinant" of the conditions on which we depend.

> In religious behavior people submit to, commit themselves to, collaborate with, or identify themselves with God as dynamic determinant in the endeavor to maintain serenity and poise in the presence of the unsatisfactory and inexorable conditions of life.[8]

Bernhardt's choice of power as the category for deity rests on this evidence.

Notice what seems to be an inconsistency, despite Bernhardt's elaborate concern for methodological correctness. Contrary to his claim that the divine as power is the starting point for natural-ism's reconstruction, his inquiry actually takes value as its point of departure. This is presupposed in the choice of functional analysis. Concern for human good in the form of serenity in the face of non-manipulable aspects of experience is the basis for Bernhardt's inquiry. The divine is construed in terms of this value; serenity is inculcated by giving devotion to the inexorable power that governs our lives. My claim that Bernhardt saw his position as pantheistic is further substantiated by the fact that he derives from the above view the ethic of consolation or *ataraxia* that usually accompanies pantheism.

It is significant that Bernhardt grants that his choice of the dynamic category as the basis for inquiry into the nature of God involves the loss of values considered important in traditional religion. Never-theless, he claims that two important values flow from this choice. The first is that conceiving God as dynamic determinant orients people to realty as a whole rather than to those aspects of reality that have value for human life. When we define deity in terms of value, he says, religious thought tends to interpret reality in a sen-timental way as supportive of human needs. In later writings, Bernhardt uses at this point in his argument Sigmund Freud's alle-gation that theistic belief humanizes nature and represents the dom-inance of the pleasure principle over the reality principle; and he insists that this applies to Wieman's view just as much as to super-naturalistic theism.[9]

The second value Bernhardt claims for his characterization of God as divine determinant is theocentricity. He says that if we see God as the source of human good this will deepen the human tendency toward egocentricity.

> The adoption of dynamic determinant as category for deity makes God as dominant power in the existential medium as a whole the primary pole in the religious relationship. . . . [R]eligious individuals measure themselves by the divine standard rather than measuring God by their needs. In this way they may achieve a truer estimate of their position in the scheme of things. The primary objection to Wieman's category of creativity . . . is that, whereas it is reality-centered, his central reality is a highly selective phase of the totality.[10]

In calling Wieman's approach reality-centered I believe Bernhardt means that he agrees with Wieman in seeing the divine naturalistically, or as absolutely immanent; Bernhardt's complaint is that Wieman's idea of creativity selects those aspects of reality fostering the fulfillment of human life.

Bernhardt summarizes the two values he claims for his approach in the assertion that it will ". . . orient us to reality *as it is* and *as a whole* rather than as we may wish it to be or as it is in part."[11] I conclude that dynamic determinant as the dominant power shaping nature and human life is simply another name for "the way things are" in nature as a whole; in short, it is a pantheistic definition of the religious ultimate. Bernhardt concludes that what follows is a religious ethic of "rugged realism," a tough-minded religion which encourages the acceptance of whatever occurs, such as he finds in the Stoicism of Epictetus and Marcus Aurelius. This is clearly the ethic of pantheism.

Naturalistic Theism: the Divine as Creativity

Wieman attempted to justify the categorization of God as the source of human good which had guided his writing for many years, in his second contribution to the published exchange.[12] He then went on to present a concept of God based on this categorization.

Bernhardt's challenge had made Wieman more self-conscious about methodology. He claims that the method of choosing the categorization of the divine "is to render explicit by analysis the category for God which is implicit in the living of the most magnificent lives in our Christian tradition."[13] The example he chooses is that of Paul the Apostle.

Persons living in this way manifest a stabilizing of life through recognition that beyond particular goods that come and go there is a creative source of good. They know that the ultimate good of life is in commitment to the creative source of good, and therefore live with a kind of detachment from particular goods this source has created, accepting suffering and loss. "In the depths of darkness and misery they seem to be aware of a creativity, and, sinking deep into its power, to die and to live under its control."[14]

This outlook and practice is for Wieman the fulfillment of human life. The category for God is the category of what works in this way in human life, what he calls creativity. Creativity is that to which

Paul practiced self-commitment, and creativity in turn produced this self-commitment within him. As a religious liberal, Wieman contends that Paul's beliefs about the divine were typical of his time, and cannot be used today because of our different cultural situation. But it is not Paul's particular beliefs about a supernatural God which brought about the saving transformation; his beliefs were simply a way of placing himself under the control of creativity. Though Paul's beliefs are not those of a religious naturalist, the divine is categoreally the same in our time as in Paul's. The divine is the creative source of the fulfillment of human life.

Having categorized the divine in terms of value, Wieman goes on to present a concept of God, asking about the nature of this creative source of transformation. He says that creativity is *most clearly seen* in a certain kind of communication; but note that this way of putting the matter implies that creativity works on all levels of the cosmos and not just in human interactions. (Here in this text from the early 'forties we see Wieman in a transition from a concern for cosmic creativity to a more exclusive emphasis on creativity in communication.)

The "four-fold working of creativity" in human communication is summarized under the headings "perspective, mentality, appreciation, and community." (1) We receive a new idea or perspective through communication with another. (2) This idea is integrated into the unique structure of our own mind, thus expanding it. (3) The world we are able to experience, understand, and appreciate is thereby expanded. (4) Community, trust, and mutual understanding increase among the participants. This concept of creative communication was to become the centerpiece of *The Source of Human Good* (1946).

We call Wieman a naturalistic *theist* because of his claim that this creativity works beyond human power to bring about changes which intentional effort could not. (1) As to "perspective" he says that we cannot seek an idea we do not have, because to seek it is already to have it, and so we must simply open ourselves to communication. (2) As to "mentality" the transformation of the mind is beyond human power, as is seen when Paul came to cherish what he formerly repudiated. (3) As to "appreciation" we cannot experience or discriminate things in experience without the requisite interpretive ideas. In an earlier essay in the series, Wieman said that a person from a technologically simple, nomadic society confronted with a chair, but lacking the concept of its meaning and use, would not experience "chair" but something else, say a piece of a tree, fuel, or a magical or an artistic object.[15] (4) Similarly as to "community" we cannot widen and deepen our present understanding of others on the basis of the present structure of our minds. So creativity does for us what we cannot do for ourselves, just as did the supernatural God of tradition.

The human contribution is merely to put ourselves more fully under the control of creativity, to set the conditions under which it can work; but what creativity will produce, no one can foresee. Wieman maintains that religious life is commitment to creativity at work in the world and in human life, and engaging in practices which encourage openness to transformation by its operation, including the willingness to sacrifice the existing order of our minds and the structure of our communities. This is again clearly the theistic stance without the transcendent God.

Wieman is usually thought to be disinterested in traditional religion. But in this exchange with Bernhardt he preserves central values of that tradition by restating his distinction between "creative good" and "created good." Created good is the presently existing results of the working of creative good in the past; it is the present state of our lives, personalities, and communities. The growth of created good is the increase of the appreciable world; we are more able to experience the qualitative richness of the world and the joys and sorrows of others, and our knowledge and freedom of choice grow. But the peace and detachment found in exemplary religious living is made possible by commitment to the creative source of these goods and a non-attachment to the present arrangement of our lives. Wieman says that religious living is to let creativity transform our loves and hates, to take from us what we once loved and to create something new.

Paradoxically, the increase of our appreciable world means the enlargement of the scope and effectiveness of our action, and thus of our ability to do evil. For Wieman, evil is the use of our magnified perspective and enhanced power to block further transformation by creativity; it is clinging to created good, as opposed to

commitment to constant transformation. The greater the good produced by creativity, the greater our power and abundance, and
Wieman believes this result may lead us to think we can live with
less reliance on creativity. The peculiar nature of creativity is that it
gives to humans all the intelligence and ability which they turn
against it, so that humans oppose the source of their own strength.
As we have seen before, in these paradoxes the religious liberal and
naturalist preserves traditional biblical insights.

To put this idea another way, at just this point Wieman is rejecting the deeply anti-traditional modernism of Bernhardt. For Bernhardt had celebrated the historical growth of human knowledge and
control as the decrease of our need of God, as conceived by both the
tradition and by Wieman.

Wieman seems to have in mind Bernhardt's emphasis on
dominant power when we characterizes the working of creativity as appearing like weakness. "So mighty is its weakness that
it has no strength at all when measured in units of human power.
So strange its goodness that we ignore it when we do not
despise, resist, or reject it."[16] The creativity at work in the evolving universe and in human life is hidden, easily overlooked,
gentle and gradual rather than dynamic and dominant. This is
why according to Wieman it is symbolized in the birth of a child
in a stable and the crucifixion of a young man. Here Wieman has
clearly described the theistic stance of openness to transformation and expectation of re-birth, in contrast to the stoical resignation of pantheism.

Objective Religious Inquiry and Wieman
as Christian Theologian

It is typical of Bernhardt's approach that he claims Wieman's mis-
takes are all methodological.[17] According to Bernhardt, in Wieman's
attempt to justify the classification of the divine as source of value
he is using what William James called "the method of extreme cases,"
which in turn is a form of "the method of simple enumeration," as
criticized by John Stuart Mill. The fallacy defined by Mill is that of
defining an hypothesis and then collecting confirmatory examples;
in the special form criticized by James, the hypothesis is derived

from some striking, well-known phenomenon. The hypothesis seems to have been confirmed, as there are no negative instances, but this is only because the evidence has not been surveyed objectively but has been selected so as to confirm and illustrate the investigator's theory. It would only take a single negative instance to undermine the explanatory power of the hypothesis.

Bernhardt is saying that Wieman has simply defined religious experience as creative transformation, as exemplified in the experience of Paul the Apostle. Then it follows that every instance of religious behavior must be an instance of creativity, and its effects must be those Wieman describes as the growth of the appreciable world. Other types of experience are overlooked because they are not confirmatory. But negative instances can be found, according to Bernhardt. Unitive mysticism is not, in Bernhardt's view, an expansion of awareness but its elimination.

It should be remembered that Wieman had a life-long interest in the study of mysticism, had discussed it in his early and latter writings, and in different ways had described the mystics' suspension of ordinary habits of interpretation and response as a phase in the transformation of the self. This account of mysticism will be examined in the next chapter. I believe Wieman could have responded along these lines regarding this particular alleged negative instance, but he did not.

Bernhardt claims there is a second methodological mistake in Wieman's justification of his characterization of God as the source of human good. This error underlies his selection of Paul as an example. The mistake is the method of initiating religious inquiry with introspection of one's own experiences, and then interpreting those of others in these terms, and finally returning to one's own with increased understanding. The approach is justified by the claim that one cannot stand outside one's own tradition and observe a variety of different religious ways as if from an objective point of view. I believe that at present, this is a widely held belief regarding dialogue between different religious traditions. But Bernhardt believes that this methodology is subjective and circular, leading to the error of thinking we have discovered the true character of religion when we have only projected outward our own understanding.

Bernhardt suggests a better method which embodies a faith in the possibility and value of "scientific objectivity," a faith which may strike the reader as naive, but that was common enough half a century ago. We should, he says, define religious experience in terms of characteristics common to all instances, thus avoiding the "highly subjective" approach which takes as normative its own understanding. The evidence of religious history is to be approached objectively and quantitatively, to escape personal bias and cultural conditioning. Wieman's method of studying "the most significant lives" introduces a qualitative and subjective factor, according to Bernhardt. In contrast, the objective and quantitative approach prevents over-emphasis on some types of evidence and is responsible for the great advances of knowledge in the modern period.

Here we have an uncritical faith in objectivity typical of an earlier era. But Bernhardt's criticism is useful for our understanding of Wieman, because it makes clear that Wieman is not really conducting an empirical investigation of religious reality *de novo*, as he seems to claim under the influence of the same scientism to which his student Bernhardt is captive. The reader will have noticed that Bernhardt and Wieman explain their beliefs as if they were conducting an empirical search for the divine. But as a matter of fact, Wieman is functioning as a Christian theologian with prior commitment to a certain understanding of the divine; his project is simply to develop a restatement of selected Christian themes in terms of the new naturalistic world-view.

This is the view of Daniel Day Williams, a former student and colleague of Wieman.

> Wieman's thought arises within the Christian community as an expression of the essential truth of the Christian faith. His development of an empirical philosophical interpretation of Christian belief has always been regarded by him as an aspect of the theological task. . . . Wieman has developed an explicit theory of the relation of his method of inquiry in religion to the Christian community and its faith, and has always shown how his conclusions may be interpreted in the light of understanding the meaning of traditional Christian doctrines.[18]

Somewhere Wieman says that the purpose of naturalistic religious philosophy is not to re-invent religion, but to interpret religious life as practiced in believing communities in terms of a changed world view. As deeply discontinuous with tradition as is

Wieman's naturalistic theism, he is in this sense a conservative, seeking to preserve and restate in a changed world the essence of theistic religion. Bernhardt is the modernist, believing that the naturalistic world-view calls for the replacement of concern for religious transformation with the ethic of stoic resignation.

The conclusion of the exchange between Bernhardt and Wieman was in the form of a letter to the editor of the *Journal of Religion*.[19] In my view, Wieman's response corresponds with the postmodern critique of objectivism and is both correct and decisive.

Wieman replies to the criticism of methodological subjectivism in a revealing way. He understands Bernhardt to have said that if creativity is the category for God, then every instance of religious behavior must be oriented toward creativity and include growth in appreciable awareness. And if he can find any religious behavior that is not an expression of creativity, Bernhardt thinks he has refuted the choice of the category of value for the divine. To Wieman, this is an erroneous view. It is just as false as saying "every instance of food-seeking behavior is oriented toward what really nourishes."[20] The way to find out the nature of God is not to find out what every person in every instance tried to worship, but what in experience is worthy of worship. Here I believe Wieman makes clear that theology is normative and not simply objective; it makes judgments of what should be and does not merely describe the variety of beliefs. Further, it is clear that he sees his work as an expression of the faith of a tradition, once again, a theologian in service of a community's belief and practice and not just a scientific inquirer.

Wieman rejects Bernhardt's "quantitative, objective" approach, which is supposed to reveal that religion is worship of the dynamic determiner of everything. When religion is found that is the worship of power, Wieman says, it must be resisted. Wieman maintains that "the fact that it is common doesn't make it excellent,"[21] and that his interest is in what is best. This again reveals that his type of religious inquiry is a normative activity.

Having replied to Bernhardt's criticism, Wieman now makes a critical comment of his own. He claims that Bernhardt's method is to find out what all people seek in all instances of religion (a task that strikes Wieman as impossible), and he observes that Bernhardt concludes that what is universally sought is serenity in the face of difficulty and danger. Next, Bernhardt searches for an idea of God which will give people what they want; and this is said to be God as dynamic determinant. "Thus he achieves an idea of God that can be utilized by people to get what they want subjectively— serenity."[22] It is odd, according to Wieman, that Bernhardt criticizes those who seek a concept of deity by way of value on the ground that this encourages egocentrism, since he appears to have done this himself. I believe that Wieman is correct: Bernhardt's interpretion of God begins with a concern for human good.

The difference between Wieman and Bernhardt is that Bernhardt interprets value as what people want as they are presently consti- tuted, namely peace of mind and contentment; whereas, according to Wieman, creativity does not fulfill our needs as we now conceive them, but transforms us so that we come to yearn for something new. Wieman defines the divine creative activity at work in the observable world as the source of human good, but this is quite dif- ferent from something that fulfills the wishes of the self as it now is. In the language used in an earlier chapter, the divine is not just the *source* of human good but its *norm*.

It is clear from this study of the Wieman-Bernhardt exchange that each participant was presenting his case for the choice of a particular interpretation of the religious ultimate, within the devel- oping school of American religious naturalism. Though the terms were not used, the issue was between Wieman's naturalistic the- ism and Bernhardt's pantheism. Bernhardt depicts the object of religious devotion as the dynamic determinant of the course of nature; religious commitment is to focus on the power shaping nature as a whole, whether it is supportive of human good or not. What follows is the ethos typical of pantheism, that of stoic accep- tance and resignation.

In contrast, Wieman's view of the object of religious devotion is a form of naturalistic theism; the divine is a term selecting for atten- tion that creativity within nature which recurrently transforms human life. The consequence of living under the guidance of this view would be openness rather than resignation. This openness includes both trusting expectation of renewal through the working of a power outside oneself, and willingness to sacrifice present good for emerging good, in short the ethos of theism.

Chapter Six

Mysticism

Wieman's naturalistic concept of the divine creative activity was always that of a process in which relations are woven between events such that the new order manifests powers not manifest in the constituents. At first he was interested in the universe-wide working of this creativity, but out of a concern to develop a concept which could guide the reorganization of life and direct decision-making, he more and more concentrated on that working of creativity in human communication which reorders the mind. Still, creative interchange embodies the same growth of relations of mutual support which creative synthesis was said to weave on all levels of being. A second shift in emphasis is seen in Wieman's rejection of the speculative metaphysical idea of the principle of concretion which appeared in his earliest attempts to reconstruct the concept of God; the idea of creative synthesis identifies a creative process observed in the world without attempting a metaphysical explanation of what brings it about. But talk about phases in Wieman's thought related to changing emphases should not obscure the more important continuities.

One of these is Wieman's phenomenology of mysticism which remained more or less constant in outline throughout his career, and which was first encountered in Chapter Three. This is the view of the moment of mystical awareness as the suspension of the system of meanings which structures and orders our experience and a reimmersion in "immediate experience." While Wieman as a naturalist always rejected William James' contention that mysticism manifests a discrete "spiritual" intuition, the concept of immediate experience is in part from James' psychology, although put to a new use by Wieman. The concern of this chapter is to show that while the description of mysticism remains the same in Wieman's writing, the meaning of this description changes as it is brought into relation with changing concepts of the divine creative activity. And this change in turn reveals an inadequacy introduced into his thought about the divine by the attempt to identify creative interchange as the sole ground of the growth of human good.

Mysticism and Progressive Integration

Wieman's most complete and satisfying discussion of mystical experience is found in *Normative Psychology of Religion* (1935), written with his second wife Regina Westcott-Wieman. The discussion in this book differs from his earlier examination of mysticism encountered above in the third chapter. There, in a way that strikes us now as somewhat naive, Wieman had used religious experience as the special datum of religious inquiry, from which concepts were to be derived and experimentally tested, yielding empirical knowledge of God. This framework is absent in his work of the 'thirties. Also, in the earlier studies Wieman maintained that the mystical experience transforms human personality because it represents a moment of radical openness to the influence of the principle of concretion, which works its subliminal persuasion on all things. In *Normative Psychology* Wieman no longer maintains that mysticism is a unique and privileged experience of a religious reality; if mystical experience leads to the renewal of the mind, it is simply because reality, including the mind, has a tendency toward new integrations, and the suspension of the present arrangement of the self in the mystical moment may allow for this tendency to work within the person.

As we will see in the concluding section of this chapter, Wieman evidently felt that this idea of openness to the creative synthesizing and integrating drift of nature was insufficient, and he attempted to account for the transformation of personality in religious life through the concept of creative communication. In doing this he would be able to claim, as he had in his earliest description of religious experience, that he had discovered a specifiable factor which operates in all religious experience. Thus, the principle of concretion adapted from Whitehead, and the idea of the event of creative communication, are alike in that they represent Wieman's drive toward specificity. The developing thesis of our study is that he should not have followed this path.

Wieman begins as before with the notion that beyond the narrow margins of our familiar world are vast realms of possible experience which may come to awareness if new ways of thinking and acting are developed. We know this because we have all undergone the expansion of our awareness of the natural world by learning a new concept through conversation or study, or by acquiring a new way of seeing through encounter with a work of art. Normally, the habitual activities that make up the personality are organized into a system that is adjusted to and finds support in some sector of the environment. This process yields our sense of the "real world." But, of course, this is just a selection out of a richer context; out of all possible-experiences, the qualities we actually experience are determined by the organization of activities that makes up our personality. If this organization changes, our world as experienced changes.

According to Wieman, the mystical experience occurs when the established organization of the personality is dissolved or suspended, so that we no longer act in such a way that we experience the familiar world. In contrast with his earlier description of this experience, Wieman now maintains that while it may lead to a new organization of the personality which is able to include experiences formerly beyond the margins of the familiar, it does not always have this effect.

Wieman's description of mystical experience is now more varied and perceptive. He says that sometimes it is characterized by a diffused awareness or a general vagueness, because of our unselective receptivity to external influences and a lack of organization in our reactions. Or the experience may be marked by bright and vivid qualities: consciousness may become a torrent of images, or one image may absorb our attention, as in the presence of a great light or a strange voice. Generally, there is a feeling of passivity, of being acted upon rather than being in control.

In one form of the experience, just because the restraints and selectivity of the established order of the personality are broken down, the subject experiences "a unitary fullness." This experience of the oneness of reality and our inclusion in it is given a characteristic explanation by Wieman. He says that our ordinary selectivity and focused attention prevent us from seeing the great wealth of functional connections of mutual support that are actually present in the world; the experience of oneness is thus a perception of the web of being that has been woven by the processes of creative synthesis. Wieman might say that this is an intuition of the order of the universe as it has thus far evolved through progressive integration.

Wieman's phenomenology goes on to include the observation that religious experience is sometimes accompanied with disorganized behavior, such as spontaneous speech or action; this represents the release of behavior usually restrained by the established organization of the personality. Related to this is peculiar ideational content, as a throng of disorganized ideas and memories begins to flow. In this state, some new idea enabling a widened perception may arise.

Wieman describes three sorts of conditions which may provoke these experiences. Some situation may arise which arouses reactions in us which the established organization of the personality cannot control, so that it is momentarily suspended. This may occur in a love relationship or a profound aesthetic experience. In a religious context this suspension may be induced by a symbol bringing to mind the vast range of possible experience which is not yet known, or, to put it another way, the great capacity of the self for transformation toward richer experience. Wieman observes that the great mystics are overwhelmed with the idea of God as supremely good, as the object of love, and as beyond ordinary experience. Here Wieman seems to interpret traditional ideas of God as intuitions of the limitless possibilities of growth implied in the processes of creative synthesis.

In a second set of circumstances, powerful suppressed impulses may be aroused which break the constraints and disorganize the reactions which are the habitual self. The powerful drive ordinarily restrained may be sexual, and this is often given a religious interpretation. Fear and anxiety, followed by good news and relief, may let flow a disorganized flood of impulses, as may the coming of a freeing insight after long struggle with a problem. Inhibition is replaced with a sense of freedom and spontaneity, there is an uprush of suppressed impulses, and normality is suspended. As before, this may mean that the person comes into relation with features of the world ordinarily overlooked.

A third set of conditions provoking religious experience involves weakening of the powers of organization in the personality; this is more than suspension of the existing organization and has greater potential for destructiveness, according to Wieman. Extreme weariness and deprivation of sleep, the influence of a crowd, drugs, or fasting, the effect of chanting and dance, all may destroy the power of the mind to organize its reactions meaningfully. Whereas the other two types of provocation to religious experience represent the increased force and quantity of reactions to be interpreted, this third class of provocations is a weakening of the organizing power itself. Despite the fact that these different sorts of incitements operate in different ways, they all may provoke the suspension of the habitual ordering of experience.

Wieman makes an important and often overlooked point in saying that these experiences do not necessarily have any religious significance. Of course, they may be and perhaps usually are given a religious interpretation. Religious traditions contain doctrines about another realm not accessible to ordinary consciousness and perhaps known only through special revelations. It is therefore predictable that the undergoing of strange states of awareness will be interpreted as contact with this other world thought to transcend the world of empirical experience. The subject will naturally overlook the hard-to-notice modifications in the organism which underlie the experience, such as deprivation of sleep or influence of a drug, and will attribute the experience to the intrusion of supernatural powers, as they are understood in the lore of a particular religion.

For Wieman, the experience has religious significance not because it is associated with religious symbols and practices, but because it contributes to the growth of good in human life and saves us from its fundamental evils. For Wieman the problem of life is the alternation of torpidity and conflict; when we arise from the stagnation of a life of habit, it is because we have fallen into difficulties of maladjustment and unsolved problems. We live in bondage to limited visions and objectives, and yet we cannot contrive new, more satisfying visions. The religious question is what can save us from this impasse? The experience Wieman has described, whatever its cause, gains religious value if it saves us from the cramping effects of the present order of our lives and their accompanying problems, and opens us outward toward an enriched experience.

> By dissolving the established organization of the personality [religious experiences] open the way to an infinite realm of possible meanings and

values, as yet unexplored, undiscriminated, and unachieved. Every
specific organization of the personality excludes this infinite realm,
because any achieved organization of the self is necessarily very limited. . . . Thus any organization of the personality cuts us off, not from
God, but from the wholeness of God. Mystical experience breaks through
this organization by dissolving it. We do not then forthwith develop new
meanings. But we open up the possibility of so doing.[1]

The mystical type of awareness gains religious value if it increases
discernment of possibilities of transcending the present order of
the self and opens us toward transformation in the direction of
greater good.

This vision of possibilities of change includes a loosening of the
hold of the present order of our lives on us; we are to an extent freed
from the fear of the loss of old meanings and patterns, and confident
in the emergence of new meanings which will create a new adjustment. Mystical experience has religious meaning when it is the experience of God, understood as the growth that is creative synthesis.

God is the infinite growth of meaning, which is not the same as progress,
but is growth which springs with new meaning out of disaster, as well as
in other times. It carries infinite possibilities, so that when established
meanings are driven out of existence and there is decline of value . . . this
infinite realm still hovers over the desolation . . . .[2]

In contrast with his claims in *The Wrestle of Religion with Truth*,
Wieman does not now claim that mysticism accomplishes this transformation through the reordering of the self under the influence of
the principle of concretion; he merely claims that religious experience is the birth of awareness of possibilities of the enlargement of
consciousness and openness to this change.

In the language of Wieman's writings from this time, he might
say that religious experience grants awareness of the limitless possibilities for growth implied in the processes of creative synthesis at
work throughout all things. While I believe this is his meaning, in
the quotation above he refers to this vision of the open future implied
in the idea of a universe of progressive integration as "the wholeness of God." This is a term from William Ernest Hocking, and, taken
as it stands, it is liable to a traditional interpretation which will mis-
lead us about Wieman. Wieman rejects Hocking's belief that the
wholeness of God is the wholeness of reality taken as the divine
mind;[3] and he would reject the Whiteheadian belief that God is a

mind including the infinite range of possibilities in a ranked order of preference, the so-called "primordial nature" of God. These meanings of the wholeness of God are not intended. What, then, is left? The wholeness of God in Wieman's thought seems to mean the limitless range of future transformations latent in the natural world when this world is seen as characterized by those tendencies termed progressive integration.

For Wieman, religious experience is the only way that a culture can maintain within itself the vision of possibilities of transformation in individuals and society. Religious experience does this by making persons aware of the ignored richness and fullness of immediate experience beyond and beneath everydayness; it releases the hold of cramping limitations and blindness which are basic to the present self.

> The free, spontaneous, relatively disorganized interplay of the minded organism with its environment during mystical experience may make possible a most wholesome reorganization of habits and patterns of living. While this interplay is going on, the old organization is somewhat dissolved, hence a new and better organization is made possible.[4]

But Wieman maintains that the religious experience may not actually involve this reorganization, but only create readiness for it. In any case, it is accompanied with a deep sense of refreshment, because the restraints, conflicts, tensions, crampings, and limitations which are part of any existing order of life have been thrown off for a time so that the return to ordinary life is accompanied with a sense of wider but still unrealized possibilities. One is aware of possibilities of transformation, and this awareness is the prerequisite for any transformation that may subsequently occur through the working of creative synthesis. Religious experience leaves us with the intuition that we live in an open universe rather than a closed one. Thus, as mentioned before, the open future and openness to possibilities of growth are forms of transcendence found in Wieman's thought.

Mysticism and Creative Interchange

If we ask the Wieman of *Normative Psychology* what will bring about the reordering of the mind and the enrichment of experience, he seems to say that this comes about where and when it does because nature and the mind manifest the tendency called creative synthesis or progressive integration. This non-specific idea of a creative tendency in all things may seem less impressive than the Whitehead-influenced claim of his earlier study of mysticism that something called the principle of concretion works in the way we are discussing. But Wieman came to believe that the feeling that we are dealing with something more than the observed when we attribute causal power to a principle is merely the beguiling effect of words.

So Wieman leaves us with a Spirit that, like the wind, blows where it will. But this conclusion was evidently unsatisfactory for Wieman, and, as we have seen, he went on to identify one event, creative interchange, as the sole and specific cause of creative transformation in human life. We turn now to Wieman's description of mysticism as he developed it in the books of his last period, especially *Man's Ultimate Commitment* (1958).

Wieman's insight that the need of human personality is to undergo constant transformation, so that we become aware of and responsive to an ever wider, deeper, and richer range of experience, continues in his later work and is thus revealed as fundamental. That Wieman is able to express this idea in a new way in his works of the 'forties and later is a sign of his own commitment to creative transformation.

The problem of religious inquiry is to identify a source of personal transformation actually and observably operating within human life, so as to be able to come into a fruitful relation with it. Wieman describes experience as a flow of felt quality, mediated to us by the system of meanings which constitutes the structure of our minds as thus far developed. Meanings are simply the patterns of interpretation and response built up by communication, through which we relate to passing experience. The fact that we undergo the expansion of the mind through development of new structures of perception suggests a rich expanse of quality which could enter experience if the mind as a system of meanings were expanded to reach more deeply into it. There is, so to speak, an ocean of quality waiting to be brought to awareness by the creation of new structures of thought.

To Wieman, the law of human development is that mind must expand so that we become increasingly aware of and responsive to an ever richer and deeper range of quality. When this law is not observed, inner conflict, boredom, a sense of meaninglessness, discontent, or guilt arise. Progress is made toward solving the problem of religious inquiry when we observe that new structures of meaning come about through a type of communication he calls creative interchange. The mind as a system of meanings mediating the experience of quality to us is the outcome of a creativity at work in communication.

Creative interchange, as Wieman now describes it, has two aspects.

> Creative interchange is that kind of interchange which creates in those who engage in it an appreciative understanding of the original experience of one another. One gets the view point of the other under such conditions that this original view derived from the other integrates with one's own personal resources. This integration modifies the view derived from the other in such a way that it becomes a part of one's own original experience.[5]

From this statement it is clear that creative interchange has two aspects, one interpersonal and the other intrapersonal.

> One aspect is the understanding in some measure of the original experience of the other person. The other aspect is the integration of what one gets from others in such a way as to create progressively the original experience which is oneself.[6]

One requisite for entering into such communication is awareness of one's own original experience beneath the layers of learned social patterns; another is candor in expressing this awareness in spite of its uniqueness and the vulnerability such expression may involve. A requirement complementary to these is that one is to be appreciative rather than judging and rejecting of what is received from the other. Further, it is necessary that what is expressed must not be intended to manipulate, impress, or demean the other; this obviates defensiveness and rejection, and increases the possibility that the meanings communicated will be accepted and integrated into the self. And finally, it is required that one be open to creative transformation through integration into the self of the meanings thus acquired; one must be ready to sacrifice the existing state of the self for that which may emerge.

Creative interchange is thus the answer to the problem of religious inquiry as Wieman defined it, because it is that structured event that actually works to transform us in the direction of fullest humanity. Wieman understands creative interchange as the operational meaning of the concept of God. In this phase of his thought, Wieman is intentionally disinterested in the cosmic aspect of creativity.

> This creativity which works between people in the form of interchange, and also within each individual, may be only a shallow, superficial manifestation of an infinite Being of mystery. It may be that this Being in its wholeness is what creates, sustains, saves, and transforms human life toward the greater good. But obviously we can make no statement about the mystery except to acknowledge it, precisely because it is a mystery. On the other hand, the creativity here under consideration can be known and studied and therefore can guide our commitment.[7]

Even if creative interchange is a manifestation of a supernatural God or a primordial cosmic ordering principle, these are in themselves beyond knowledge, according to Wieman, and we are left with the observable manifestation, a creativity active in mind and communication. The value of this concept is, according to the Wieman of this later period, that it can guide decision and action, in that we can seek to create conditions in ourselves and society necessary to the operation of creativity when it is conceived in this concrete way.

Contrasted with his first studies of mysticism in the late 'twenties, discussed in Chapter Three, Wieman has reconceived the source of personal transformation toward greater appreciative awareness; the power operating in this change is not the principle of concretion but the event of creative interchange. Nevertheless, the analysis of mysticism found in the early work and his writings of the 'thirties is retained. In the terms of *Man's Ultimate Commitment*, the mystical experience is an ecstatic awareness of the immense richness of quality beyond the reach of the present structures of mind, which arises because of the momentary suspension of the mediating function of these structures. It is thus literally immediate experience. Awareness of this qualitative richness beyond and beneath the limits of experience as presently structured calls for the development of new structures of perception, new meanings, ideas, habits, attitudes, institutions, and customs. But the actual transformation of the mind comes about not in the mystical experience but through the process of creative interchange. The mystic grasps the possibility of a qualitatively richer experience beyond the reach of present meanings and instigates communication which leads to the transformation of minds, first within a small circle of initiates and often spreading culture-wide. In contrast with his first studies and like his work of the 'thirties, Wieman claims that mystical awareness is not itself the point of transformation of the mind; he now goes on to define the creative factor as the interaction of the community in which it occurs.

Since the experience of the encompassing qualitative richness cannot be grasped in presently available words and ideas, it is literally ineffable, and the mystic therefore refers to the experience as immersion in "the eternal." But in Wieman's view, what is experienced is not "outside time," for in his empiricism nothing outside of time can be experienced.

We might ask if there is an "unknown structure of reality" behind the flow of felt quality, and if this is the eternal of which the mystic speaks. In his somewhat Whiteheadian phase, Wieman answered affirmatively. But the empiricist strand in Wieman's thought now leaves no room for such speculations, and he asserts that "reality" is the flow of felt quality, and "structure" is a human mental construct selecting parts of this richness for discrimination and attention. On these terms, "unknown structure of reality" is a meaningless combination of words, equivalent to nothing.

Or we might ask if creative interchange is the manifestation on the level of human life of a creativity operating on all levels of existence. I do not believe that Wieman ever denies this, but he became less and less interested in this cosmic dimension, and more and more absorbed in the idea that human life is fulfilled in and through creative interchange. The long evolution which gave rise to sensitive, symbol-using organisms is the work of something like what he had called creative synthesis, but that working of creativity which brings life to fulfillment is the reordering of the mind through communicated meanings. Interest in the continued manifestation of progressive integration in our bodies and our world, in hidden and manifest ways, would draw our interest away from what Wieman came to regard as an important discovery, creative communication.

The Quest for Specificity

Aside from providing an intriguing and fruitful phenomenology of mysticism, the study of Wieman's understanding of mysticism makes possible a clearer discrimination of his shifting, developing understanding of the naturalistic meaning of God. In *The Wrestle of Religion with Truth*, mystical awareness is a moment of receptivity and possible atunement to an order pervading the natural world making for progressively richer concretions of experience. Openness to the divine conceived as the principle of concretion enables the self to prehend the universe more richly and fully. In *Normative Psychology of Religion* the mystical moment is awareness of the creative character of nature, opening up endless possibilities of growth and relativizing the present order of our lives; this aware-ness constitutes readiness for whatever transformation may arise through the operation of creative synthesis in and around us. In *Man's Ultimate Commitment*, mysticism is similarly described as an awakening to the wealth of experience beyond the reach of the mind as presently constituted, but the creative factor in transforming the mind toward greater appreciative awareness is not the pervasive creativity of nature but a specifiable, event, namely the creative-interchange which takes place in the community into which the mys-tical experience breaks.

This is the first time in our study that the idea of creative syn-thesis or progressive integration has been juxtaposed with the more specific concept of creative communication. Wieman's concern was to specify the one event involved in every instance of the growth of good in human life, so as to give concrete guidance to human action. He has claimed that whatever theory of value we adopt, an increase of awareness, a widening and deepening of our appreciable world, will increase the good of human life.

Does the event of creative interchange do this? In a sense he set-tles this matter by definition rather than through his empirical method; that is, he includes expansion of the sector of reality we are capable of discerning and enjoying as part of creative interchange.[8] We might say that this simply manifests creative synthesis as it occurs within the mind, since every instance of creativity is a bringing together of parts, in this case perspectives or interpretations in the mind, so that they form new wholes which function with wider scope. What is actually gained in the narrower concept of creative interchange? Just that the meanings recombined by the process of the mind's progressive integration come from communication. Wieman has not proven empirically that this is so, or that, if meanings received in communication are essential, they must be given and received in a certain spirit. What is actually creative is the mind's recombining and synthesizing, which is an instance of the process of creative synthesis.

And while it is dubious that anything is gained, perhaps something is lost by Wieman's persistent quest for specificity. It would seem that what is required for the working of creativity in transforming the mind is religious practices which both encourage the letting-go of existing created good and provide a vision of boundless possibilities of expansion and renewal. This might be provided for some by traditional religious beliefs and practices, and for others, by a re-interpretation of these beliefs and practices through naturalistic concepts like creative synthesis. If we focus instead on communication in the belief that this is the sole way in which good grows, the breadth of our vision is narrowed; our openness to creative synthesis, which works as, when, and where it will, will be blocked by self-conscious preoccupation with communication. Single- minded concentration on creativity in communication may prevent openness to the variety of unpredictable manifestations of creativity elsewhere. I conclude that nothing is really gained and something is lost by Wieman's drift from the religious to the psychological realm in his attempt to understand creativity.

Wieman is at his best when he reminds us that, after all, religious commitment is not to be given to any concept of the divine creative activity, including his own idea of creative interchange. Rather, commitment is to be given to creativity itself, which must always be more than any concept of it. This is in keeping with his instrumentalist view of ideas as guiding us into relations rather than disclosing the inner nature of things. Taking his advice, we may conclude that his contribution does not lie in the "discovery" of creative interchange; instead, the import of his work is to encourage a generalized but intense openness to nature's grace.

Chapter Seven

Christology

The work of reinterpreting the basic themes of Christian theology was a life-long concern of Wieman, but the only extended
discussion of the originating events of Christianity occurs in
Wieman's writings of the 'fifties and later. Here he developed an
interpretation of the ministry of Jesus of Nazareth and its personal
and historical effect which centers on the concept of creative interchange. In these works of his last period the claim that the need of
life is for constant growth, what we might call his process view of
the self, is most fully stated.

Creative Communication and Unitarianism of the Third Person

The reader will recall that the central concept of this later phase of
Wieman's work is that of the divine as creative interchange, an event
in interpersonal communication which transforms the self toward
fuller actualization. This event was intended as an empirical and
naturalistic content for the concept of God. The uniqueness of
Wieman's thought is precisely this attempt to rethink the notion of
the divine within the framework of the non-reductive naturalism
current in American philosophy in the first half of this century.

Even in these writings of most recent date, Wieman continues to
present his ideas in the form of an empirical inquiry. As before, he
asserts that the primary question for religious inquiry is "what can
actualize most completely the constructive potentialities of human
existence?"[1] Restating a recurrent theme, Wieman says that our most
fundamental drive is the desire to bring the whole of our being into
active engagement with life, rather than living entirely on the level
of that fraction of the self which present conditions will permit of
realization.[2] Clinging to existing orders of life for security conflicts

with this drive, generating discontent. This discontent involves both
an awareness of unrealized potentialities and an awareness of the
human capacity for radical transformation.[3] This situation gives rise
to the religious problem, which is ". . . to find a way of life fitted to
the potentialities of human existence, to release them most fully with
constructive power."[4]

Our discontent forces upon us the knowledge that we are not at
home in our world as it is now ordered. "Every organization of life
which we set up, or enter, becomes in time like a prison to us, so
that we must strive to break free of it, and in this striving to break
free of it, we break it down."[5] The demands of our natures are such
that they cannot be met in any existing order of life, and thus they
call for a continuous creative reorganization of the self and society.
Here we have a clear statement of what we may call Wieman's concept of the self as process rather than as substance.

The required transformation cannot be the result of the human
effort to implement the best available plans or to apply to life our
highest values, because it requires the creation of new plans and
values which could not be imagined on the present level of life. Thus,
Wieman rejects moral activism as an approach to the problem of life;
as embodied in secular humanism, this approach ignores the need
for creative transformation beyond present levels of insight. Here
Wieman asserts the primacy of the religious approach over the
ethical. Further, the source of any transformation from the existing
order cannot be found beyond nature. Wieman's naturalism is seen
in his insistence that we cannot find the source of that life which
satisfies the needs of our being beyond nature in a realm of transcendence, because our knowledge is limited to experience of this
world of events. Transformation must be seen as the result of a
creativity actually operative in human life, within nature.

The religious problem as conceived by Wieman can now be fully
stated: "what operates in human life with such character and power
that it will transform us as we cannot transform ourselves, to save
us from the depths of evil and endow us with the greatest good,
provided that we give ourselves over to it with whatsoever com-
pleteness of self-giving is possible for us."[6] The solution to the
religious problem will be in commitment to that creativity actually
and observably operative in human life. This creativity, whatever

its nature be found to be, will be the religious ultimate or the naturalistic meaning of God.

The religious problem is thus to find that in human experience which transforms us as we cannot transform ourselves, so that an ever greater part of the self's potentialities are brought into interaction with an ever wider and fuller environment. That which actually operates in such a way is, according to the later Wieman, a certain kind of communication between persons. Creative interchange is the answer to the religious problem, in that the creative transformation necessary to the greatest good of human life is actually observed to occur as a result of a certain kind of interchange among persons.

> In its most complete form it can be described thus: You express your whole self and your entire mind freely and fully and deeply and truly to other persons who understand you most completely and appreciatively with joy in what you are as so expressed; and you yourself respond to others who express themselves freely and fully and deeply and truly while you understand them most completely and appreciatively with joy in the spirits they are.[7]

The basic claim seems to be that the unique perspective of each is shared with the other, and each is changed in the process.

Why is this the solution to the religious problem? The basis of Wieman's answer is found in the more analytic description of creative interchange as "the four-fold creative event" we encountered in his exchange with Bernhardt and in his major work *The Source of Human Good*. The event of creative interchange is said to consist of four sub-events. Through creative interchange, (1) new meanings are acquired, and (2) they are integrated with old, (3) creatively expanding the mind and the world it is able to appreciate and (4) creating community among minds. The mind is constituted by the acquiring of meanings through creative interchange with other persons, and through the integration of these meanings into a whole. Further, the extension of the system of meanings is the creation and expansion of the world it is able to appreciate. Through the generation of meaning, one becomes aware of what was hidden before, and wider and deeper ranges of experience open up. Finally, through creative interchange, minds come to share experiences and become capable of appreciating different perspectives on the world. Community is built as one comes to share the thoughts and feelings of others and to view the world from their standpoint, and this, in turn, facilitates further interchange.

As we saw in the previous chapter, this is not as much of an empirical discovery as Wieman claims. The creative event is the source of the needed expansion of the mind just because this expansion is included as the third phase of the event. And if we ask what causes this expansion, we cannot say that it is the first sub-event alone, the communication of meanings. Rather, it is the whole process, which includes the mysterious creativity of mind; and this, in turn, is an instance of a creativity at work on all levels of existence, giving rise to life and mind in the first place. Wieman's claim that empirical inquiry has specified the one root of religious change seems weak. If the special claim about creative communication is set aside, what remains is the essential tenet of naturalistic theism as elaborated in Wieman's writings of the 'thirties: life is fulfilled through the working of a creativity manifest on all levels of the evolving world and in the human mind, to the extent that we are willing to sacrifice the present order of life to the emergence of a renewed self.

In any case, Wieman maintained in his later writings that creative interchange is the answer to the problem of religious inquiry as he had formulated it, in that, when we commit ourselves to creative interchange, it transforms in the direction of the fullest actualization of human potential. Religious commitment to this creativity is the precondition which makes possible the realization of the greatest good of human life.[8] Commitment to creativity would mean the effort to provide those conditions within oneself and within society which foster creative interchange between persons, so that the creative event may occur and continue to transform human life toward the greater good. On the personal level, those conditions necessary for the continued operation of creativity are openness to creative transformation, that is, a readiness to sacrifice the existing organization of the self and society to the newly emerging organization, and sensitivity to the meanings communicated by others.[9]

As the answer to the religious problem, creative interchange is the religious ultimate or the divine. As we have seen before, in Wieman's naturalism creative interchange is taken as the actual, operative reality intended by the symbol of the supernatural, personal God.

While holding that creative interchange is a natural and wholly immanent creativity, Wieman nevertheless claims that this event has several characteristics of the transcendent, personal God of traditional religion. Creative interchange creates mind and personality, and works to unfold human potentials and establish the greatest good of human life. It saves from the greatest evils (understood as discontent, inner conflict, stagnation, and the concomitant guilt) which arise when the need of constant transformation is denied. Wieman even claims that creative interchange is that which is sinned against, because he sees sin as resistance to transformation and clinging to existing states of the self and society.

Wieman's declining interest in the idea of cosmic creativity is seen in his claim in these later writings that creative interchange may even be said to create the universe, in the special sense that it makes possible whatever experience we can have of the universe. That is, it creates mind and thus the world relative to mind, which is the appreciable world. But creative interchange is an interpersonal event and not the creator of the physical cosmos, although Wieman does not deny that it may be a manifestation on the human level of a creativity operative on other levels of the universe and visible in its evolution. But now Wieman claims that such speculation draws our attention away from the world of experience and action, whereas the value of the concept of creative interchange is precisely that it is applicable as a guide in personal and social decisions. For the later Wieman, the empirical availability provided by his concept of the divine creative activity is of more importance than the satisfaction derived from the vision of creative interchange as a form of participation in cosmic creativity.

Wieman characteristically grants that it may be that creativity works not only on all levels of existence, but is a manifestation of something beyond nature. He grants that the depth and fullness of creativity may be beyond what he has described as the creative event of communication. But in his belief all we can know of such a reality is what we can discover of creativity operative in human experience.

All attempts to find what should command the ultimate commitment by peering into the depths and heights of Being outside of human life, or into eternity or the supernatural, is to seek it where it can never be found. What

transforms human life toward the best possible must operate in human
life and in time, where humanity is, not in an eternity where it is not.[10]

The limitations placed on Wieman's thought by his empiricism are
now most evident. He concludes that we must not seek deliverance
in a mystery beyond understanding, or in a creativity discerned in
the non-human phases of existence, but in that creativity which is
observably operative in human life and thus accessible to inquiry.
In this way, he says we will actually be able to study the conditions
required for the operation of that creativity which saves and transforms, and make the required adjustments. Only commitment to a
creativity which is a character of known events can direct our action.

When we compare Wieman's concept of the divine as creative
interchange to the structure of the trinitarian dogma, Wieman
appears as a "unitarian of the third person."[11] For the purposes of
shedding light on Wieman's thought, we can take the trinitarian
idea as asserting that God is transcendent over nature as the Father,
is creatively and redemptively active in nature and human history
as the Logos, and is present and at work in the life of the Christian
community as the Spirit. Then criticism of the trinitarian dogma can
be seen as leading to three kinds of unitarian belief; each form would
involve the exclusive assertion of one aspect of the dogma and the
denial of meaning to the other two. Thus, there might be a unitarianism of the Father, a unitarianism of the Son or the Logos, and a
unitarianism of the Holy Spirit.

Unitarianism of the first person is seen in deism, the belief in a
transcendent ground of existence which is not present in the cosmos
or involved in human life, the Father without the Logos or the Spirit,
so to speak. Unitarianism of the second person might refer to belief
in a divine activity present in and through all things but not transcendent of them, something like the Logos without the Father. This
would be a wholly immanent God active throughout the natural
world and in exemplary lives.

Then the idea of God as manifest in creative interchange would
be third-person unitarianism, because it locates the divine wholly
in human life and lacks a sense of the divine transcendence over
both nature and human history. To identify the divine solely
with creative interchange is to locate the divine in the fellowship
of the church (the work of the Spirit), and to neglect the claims

that God transcends nature as the Father and acts throughout nature as the Logos.

Creative interchange is a creativity active in human groups; it is a concept of saving power at work in the community of those who practice commitment to it, a pervasive power of healing and fulfillment at work wherever two or three are gathered together. It is a counterpart of the traditional concept of the Holy Spirit at work in the community of believers.

In Wieman's concept of the divine in the writings under discussion, there is nothing corresponding to the first person of the trinity, conceived as the transcendent ground of existence. Further, the concept of creative interchange does not refer to the creative source of the pre-human, physical world; thus it does not extend as far as the concept of the second person of the trinity. Wieman has clearly presented a concept of the divine as immanent in a certain kind of human community based on acceptance and trust, as an active power at work in nourishing and building up the human spirit. Thus, creative interchange as a concept of the divine corresponds with what Christians have called the third person of the trinity and does not include anything relating to the first person. But since Wieman had something to say about the relevance of creative interchange to the Logos and Jesus of Nazareth, we must now turn to aspects of his thought which relate to the idea of the second person.

The Christ-Event

Wieman's concept of creative interchange can be applied to questions of christology and soteriology, and indeed when this is done, insights valuable for understanding Christian faith emerge. However, the concept of creative interchange was not developed as an interpretation of the meaning of the person and work of Jesus, nor of the Logos doctrine. Therefore, it is correct to say that in Wieman's discussions of Jesus, primarily found in *The Source of Human Good*, he is applying an already developed concept to the task of interpreting Jesus. This stands in contrast with his reference to the faith of Jesus and of Paul in the debate with Bernhardt over pantheism. There Christian themes were normative, defining for Wieman the essentially religious attitude of trust in creativity and non-attachment to created good. In the following, I think it will be evident that Christian themes are *illustrative* of Wieman's idea of creative communication and not *normative* for his thinking.

For Wieman in these later works, the life of Christ is not the norm of belief; what is normative is what he calls empirical inquiry. The concept of creative interchange is derived from modern philosophical inquiry, especially the idea of shared experience in the thought of John Dewey. With this concept in hand, it is possible to give an illuminating account of the transforming power at work in the circle of Jesus. But, in the phrase of Bernard Loomer, a student, colleague, and sympathetic critic of Wieman, "in Wieman's matured thought the figure of Jesus Christ seems illustrative rather than wholly constitutive."[12]

Yet, application of the concept of creative interchange to the interpretation of the person and work of Jesus is not forced or artificial, because, again in Loomer's words, "Wieman's concern has been soteriological throughout."[13] This concern is seen in what I have called the formal definition of God above; the concept of creative interchange is an answer to the question of what saves and fulfills human life. Indeed, as we have seen, Daniel Day Williams goes further and interprets Wieman not as a philosopher of religion, but as a Christian theologian absorbed in the problem of developing a contemporary interpretation of the fundamental Christian experience of encounter with a God who heals and saves.

When Wieman's concept of the divine is applied to questions of christology and soteriology, Jesus is interpreted as a person, especially but not uniquely able to facilitate creative interchange in the circle about him.

> Jesus engaged in intercommunication with a little group of disciples with such depth and potency that organization of their several personalities was broken down and they were remade. They became new persons, and the thought and feeling of each got across to the others.[14]

Wieman maintains that this was not something which Jesus did intentionally.

> It was something that happened when he was present like a catalytic agent. . . . Something about this man Jesus broke the atomic exclusiveness of those individuals so that they were deeply and freely receptive and responsive each to the other.[15]

Setting aside traditional beliefs about the revelation of the transcendent God in Jesus, Wieman maintains that the divine element
in the Christ-event was creative interchange.

> The disciples in fellowship with Jesus did not find a vision of eternal being.
> They found in that fellowship a kind of interchange which transformed
> their lives. . . . It was a transformation of their actual, concrete existing
> selves; and this transformation they passed on to others by the same kind
> of interchange they had when in fellowship with Jesus.[16]

For Wieman, the meaning of Jesus is his ability to bring about this
interchange, and not any particular content of his teaching. The
creative event in the circle around Jesus does not consist in his com-
municating his teaching to them, but in the fact that creative power
was released in the midst of this group. It was the quality of Jesus'
communication, and not the content of it, which counted.

> The saving power of his communication did not lie in any clear state-
> ment of any . . . doctrines. Rather the transforming power of the com-
> munication must have been in its quality, namely, that quality by which
> it enabled each to enter into deep appreciative awareness of the
> individuality of others and thereby acquire from them the values which
> could be progressively integrated into a depth and fullness of vision
> transforming their lives.[17]

This kind of communication is present in all human life at a low
level; in Jesus and his disciples it rose to the level of a great transforming power.

Rejecting the theme of the "religion of Jesus" movement in the
older liberal theology of Adolf Harnack and others, Wieman maintains that neither the teachings nor the personality of Jesus have
power to transform history as Jesus has. Only events can have such
power; the teachings and personality of Jesus were ingredients in the
event, but it was the total impact of the creative event of communication which gave power to his personality and teaching in history.

Wieman had always maintained that creative interchange accomplishes more than can be consciously planned or intended, because
it transforms consciousness, bringing about what could not be fore-
seen or imagined. Applied to the Christ-event, this means that the
creative transformation of persons in the circle surrounding Jesus
was "not the work of the man Jesus." Though he was essential to it,

he did not plan it by his own intelligence. Living when he did, he was not consciously aware of the nature of creative interchange.

> If Jesus had been able to understand what was taking place, his mind would not have been human, and, hence, he would not have been a human being. Salvation through Christ is not a human work, not even of the man Jesus. It is the work of God, the creative event, working through history to win dominance in human life, this dominance culminating in the life of Jesus, his death, and the Resurrection, with the consequent forming of a fellowship of faith to carry the new way of living through subsequent ages.[18]

In Wieman's christology, Jesus is fully human and is called the Christ because he founded a community in which the creative event and its transforming power are the center of commitment; in this way he began to bring into history the Kingdom of God.

Wieman's description of the precise character of the creative power centering in Jesus and his followers utilizes his familiar notion of the four-fold creative event. Those involved in creative interchange in his circle were led to a mutual awareness of and responsiveness toward the needs and interests of one another. The thought and feeling derived from others was integrated into each participant's consciousness, and thus each was transformed, each became better able "to understand, to appreciate, to act with power and insight." The appreciable world of each was expanded. "Since they could now see through the eyes of others, feel through their sensitivities, and discern the secrets of many hearts, the world was more rich and ample with meaning and quality."[19] And lastly, greater breadth and depth of community arose between them, which is the founding of the church. This creative event is the saving, transforming power at the center of Christian faith. And the power is not in *Jesus*, though he was essential to its operating in this instance; rather, he was in *it*. This is why I have used the term "Christ- event" for the originating occasion of Christian history, although Wieman does not use this term; the Christ-event includes Jesus' person, its impact on others, and the response of his followers, all in an ongoing process.

In the evangelical strand of the New Testament elaborated especially in the letters of Paul the Apostle, central importance is given to the death and resurrection of Jesus. While Wieman's approach continues the emphasis of this tradition on personal transformation, his concept of creative interchange as the key to the meaning of Jesus would not seem to give special importance to Jesus' death and resurrection. Wieman does, however, discuss these themes. In brief, the death and resurrection of Jesus mean that the creative power encountered in the circle around Jesus was experienced as continuing to operate in the group founded by him, as long as the central commitment of that little society was to that defenseless mutuality which is the precondition of creativity.

In Wieman's view, during the life of Jesus creative interchange was bound within the limits of Jewish religion and culture. Jesus was then seen as the fulfillment of the Jewish messianic hope. But the crucifixion disclosed that Jesus would not in fact fulfill the role of liberator of the Jews and restorer of their national life. It seemed that Jesus was not the expected messiah, and the disciples fell into despair. But then the power of creative transformation was surprisingly found to be at work again among the disciples.

> That kind of interaction which Jesus had engendered among them came back. They found themselves interacting with one another and with other people in that marvelous way which had only happened when Jesus was in their midst. This was the resurrection.[20]

> The life-transforming creativity previously known only in fellowship with Jesus began again to work in the fellowship of the disciples. It was risen from the dead. Since they had never experienced it except in association with Jesus, it seemed to them that the man Jesus himself was actually present, walking and talking with them. Some thought they saw him and touched him in physical presence. But what rose from the dead was not the man Jesus; it was creative power. It was the living God that works in time. It was the Second Person [sic] of the Trinity. It was Christ the God, not Jesus the man.[21]

The death of Jesus disengaged the power of creative interchange from the cultural limitations of its origin, and the resurrection is the discovery that the creative event is manifest apart from the physical presence of Jesus. Wieman sees the spread of Christianity to gentile lands in the Book of Acts and the letters of Paul as the direct result of this disentangling of the community of faith from a single cultural perspective.[22]

Notice that, in Wieman's view, what is resurrected is not the body of Jesus, but the power of creative interchange; the resurrection is thus an event in the lives of the disciples. Jesus initiated a powerful kind of creative interaction, which appeared to be absent and discredited after the crucifixion. "But now, after it had seemed to be destroyed by his death, it rose again from the dead and was with them."[23] That creativity formerly dependent on Jesus' physical presence was now known to be at work in the world through the church, and this realization liberated the power of creativity for operation in a wider sphere.

Wieman's theological liberalism is seen in his view of the physical resurrection, that is, the empty tomb and the resurrection appearances, as myth. Since the creative power experienced anew by the disciples had been associated with the physical person of Jesus, his appearance and presence were "seen and felt" by the renewed disciples. But the meaning of the resurrection myth is not the empty tomb, but the continuing power of creativity. Thus the "Living Christ" of the Pauline letters is the continuing creative power of the Christian community.

It should now be clear that Wieman is able to find meaning in the concept of "salvation by faith in Christ." Creative interchange is always at work on some minimal level in human life, but rarely is it consciously discriminated or made the dominant commitment of living. Wieman sees sin as the domination of the presently constituted will over creative transformation, as the state of holding to the existing state of the self. Then salvation would be the reversal of devotion so that the creative event comes to be the overriding commitment. And salvation is by grace and not works, in the sense that this transformation cannot be willed, but is itself the incipient work of creativity. Faith is manifest when the creative event is "lifted to dominance over other concerns,"[24] and such a faith arose in an historically effective way in the early church. Commitment to the Living Christ as the transforming power of creativity, and reliance upon creativity to fulfill life, is saving faith. Continuation of this commitment is effected by ritual, myth, and scripture which, while giving no conscious knowledge of creativity, convey the sense of its importance and evoke attitudes of trust, openness to change, and mutual love which are necessary to its operation. Through these vehicles, historical continuity is given to that commitment to creative interchange which originated in the group of men and women which centered on Jesus.

Passages from Wieman above have distinguished Jesus of Nazareth and the Christ, the second person of the trinity. By the Christ, Wieman means the power of creative interchange at work in human life, which was manifest in the community founded by Jesus. The importance of Jesus is that from him flows a historically continuous community in which commitment to creative transformation is practiced.

> Christ, as here understood, is not merely the man Jesus. Christ is the domination by the creative event over human life in a fellowship made continuous in history. Through this domination Christ is the revelation of God to humanity, the forgiveness of sin extended to all men, and the salvation of the world.... God incarnate in these creative events, and not the human nature of the man, is the Christ revealing God, forgiving sin, and saving the world.[25]

> Let me state that I do not think of Jesus as the highest product of the creative process. The revelation of God in Christ should never be identified with the man Jesus. The revelation of God is the transforming power which operated in the fellowship with Jesus and continued to operate in the fellowship of the early church, and still continues to operate today when required conditions are present. This transforming power is the Christ, the revelation of God. Christ, in this sense, can be with us here and now as truly as he was in Galilee. The transforming power, I repeat, is not the man, even through the man may have been one of the necessary conditions for the rise of this power to such dominance over counter processes as to be rightly called the revelation of God.[26]

Wieman maintains here, and I believe correctly, that the Council of Chalcedon (A.D. 451), which established the christology of orthodox Christianity, did not claim that "Jesus is God" in the simple sense; only the divine nature in Jesus Christ was God. Wieman thus asserts, "the man Jesus is not divine and is not God."[27]

As to the "divine nature" of Jesus Christ, it would be more characteristic of Wieman to set aside the static Greek philosophical language of "substance" and "nature," and to assert that Jesus the man *manifests* the divine as creativity. Wieman's view of Jesus seems to be that he has one "nature," if the term is to be used, and that nature is human. This would seem to be the Socinian christology, in which Jesus is the human messiah, the man manifesting the divine saving activity. And this appears to be so in spite of Wieman's use, in *The Source of Human Good*, of traditional language regarding the trinity and his relating of his views to Chalcedonian orthodoxy.

What is revealed in Jesus Christ is the saving power of God, which for Wieman is the power of creative interchange. Thus faith in creative communication is the substance of Christianity.

> What then is God as revealed in Jesus Christ? God as revealed in Jesus Christ is the transforming, saving power of this kind of communication which creates appreciative understanding of one another and transmits the values of one to the other.[28]

But this "revelation in Jesus Christ" cannot be propositional, for it could not be expressed in the form of doctrines by Jesus or his disciples, because there was as yet no language or body of knowledge adequate to the task. "It could be transmitted to others only in the form of a transformed life."[29] This new life was expressed in symbols, myths, ceremonies, and disciplines, and was tangibly present in the Christian community; but in Wieman's view there could not be as yet any set of propositions describing this revealed reality.

Wieman's liberalism is again evident in his contention that only in the present are we able to develop a language fit to express the nature of this operative power. Wieman feels that this is the result of the growth of self-consciousness through the modern drama and novel, and through psychology and the social sciences.[30] And it is clear that it is this modern conception of creative interchange which plays the normative role in Wieman's thought. Wieman asserts that the creative event is not divine because it is associated with Jesus; rather, it is divine only because it can be shown to manifest that saving power which is essential to the fulfillment of life.

> This creativity is called divine, not because it is revealed in Jesus Christ, or because it has powerfully shaped the religion of the western world. Rather, the reverse: What is revealed in the fellowship of Jesus can be called divine only if empirical evidence indicates that it does, in truth, have saving power.[31]

Wieman's concept of empirical theology is thus normative in this phase of his thought, and the Christ-event is illustrative. The concept of the creative event is, in Wieman's thought, applied to the problem of interpreting the events surrounding Jesus; it is not derived from them. This observation is not intended as a criticism of Wieman but only as a description of his method, for the same might be said of the Jewish, gnostic, and Hellenistic mystery themes applied to Jesus by the early church.

The view of Wieman as a unitarian of the third person is related to his strict distinction between the Christ as creativity and Jesus of Nazareth as manifesting this creativity. For Wieman intermittently refers to the Living Christ, that creativity active in the church, as the Holy Spirit.[32]

> In the Christian religion the name of Christ or Holy Spirit is given to this creativity which creates and expands the appreciative consciousness. It is sometimes called divine grace. In any case, whatever names are used, it creates love and community and more profound appreciative understanding between individuals and peoples.[33]

Creative interchange refers to a healing, whole-making presence in the community of faith, and thus corresponds with the concept of the Spirit, which in traditional belief comes to fulfill and build-up the community founded by Jesus.

The revelation of the divine in Christ has been the basis of Christian exclusivism in the past; it was believed that since God is present in Christ in a unique way, non-Christian religious traditions are at best merely humanly contrived anticipations of Christianity and, at worst, distortions and counterfeits of religious truth. The fact that for Wieman's thought the concept of creative interchange is normative and the Christ-event illustrative of it, is seen in his rejection of exclusivism. In Christianity, the centrality of commitment to creativity which first arose in the earliest Christian communities is perpetuated throughout history. But creative interchange has always operated outside of Christianity, and other communities have existed in which it was fostered; in these communities as in Christianity, explicit knowledge of the concept of creativity would be lacking, and commitment would be guided by custom and symbol. Thus, in Wieman's belief, Christianity is not unique in its essence, but only in its historical continuity and "world transforming efficacy."[34]

It seems clear that Wieman's portrait of Jesus of Nazareth is not presented as the result of historical research, but as his theological attempt to account for the transforming power radiating from the circle of Jesus' disciples. This should not be taken as a criticism of Wieman, for his approach is one of a long history of instances of the interpretation of Jesus through concepts and thought forms of a particular time and place; in Wieman's thought, Jesus is interpreted through concepts derived from the contemporary understanding of mind and communication. But the values embodied are the same mutuality and acceptance which were the marks of the first Christian communities. In any case, this tradition of applying independently derived concepts to the problem of interpreting the historical Jesus and his impact had begun already in the New Testament church itself, and continued through a long history.

Creative Synthesis and the Logos

A christology is typically not merely an interpretation of the historical Jesus but includes the claim that the creativity manifest in Jesus is a disclosure of the creativity at work in the cosmos at large.

Wieman repeatedly distinguishes between Jesus of Nazareth as one whose commitment to creativity fostered creative interchange in the circle about him, and the Christ as a larger creativity at work before, after, and apart from the life of Jesus. However, it is necessary to recall that for Wieman the Christ means creative interchange, a certain type of human interaction. The creative event is not the creator of the pre-human physical world, but operates within human communication to create mind as a system of meanings; it creates the universe known to us, our appreciable world, but not the pre-human physical universe.

> The revelation of the saving power of God in the form of creative interchange has been called the "Word" with a capital "W." In the beginning was the Word, and the Word was with God, and the Word was God. It is not called the Word because written in a book. It is called the Word because it created the human level of existence in the beginning and continues to operate in our midst with saving and transforming power when required conditions are present. It is personified because it cannot occur except between persons and in persons. . . . The living Word is operating here in our midst, not beyond history but in history, ready to rise up with saving and transfiguring power when required conditions are met.[35]

I doubt that Wieman is correctly relating his idea of creative interchange and the Logos doctrine in this passage and others quoted above. As Wieman uses the term, the Word or the second person of the trinity transcends its manifestation in Jesus, but notice that when it is interpreted as creative interchange we cannot say that the Word transcends nature or even that it operates beyond human history. As I argued in the first section of this chapter, if the creativity Wieman wants us to see works only in human groups through communication, it is more nearly like the Spirit than the Word.

The pragmatist empiricism increasingly dominant in Wieman's later period creates a reticence to speak of creative interchange as manifesting cosmic creativity. But this is just what the Word is. I have suggested that if the divine is the event of creative communication only, then Wieman is a unitarian of the third person; and this implies that creative interchange is really not at all like the traditional doctrine of the Logos, despite the above quotation. The Word as the divine creative activity working on all levels of existence is just what is absent or de-emphasized in these later studies of Wieman. For a parallel to the doctrine of the Word as the creative activity at work throughout the universe we would have to turn to his work of the 'thirties. The Logos as that through which everything was made is similar to the concept of creative synthesis, which refers to the congeries of processes of progressive integration manifest in cosmic evolution as well as in human history, and in the human body as well as the mind.

In that period, perhaps we could say Wieman was a unitarian of the second person, or at least that he had something to say that was relevant to the Logos doctrine. Then he possessed a vision of the divine creative activity as working before and beyond and not just within human society. And the absence in the writings encountered in this chapter of this vision of the divine creative activity as universe-wide in scope limits Wieman's ability to interpret the historical Jesus. It was precisely such a universal vision which seems in fact to have aroused that openness to transformation and disengagement from existing goods which are the preconditions of creative interchange in Jesus and his followers. To use the language of the sayings of Jesus in the Gospels, love of the other is the outcome of a kind of self-forgetfulness which is based on knowledge of the parental love of God for each person. Could Jesus and his circle have abandoned themselves to creative interchange if they lacked the sense of that enveloping grace which Wieman earlier had called creative synthesis? If we answer this question negatively, we must conclude that Wieman's quest for the one specifiable event on which human good depends was a fall from an earlier, more religiously adequate vision.

Conclusion

In his quest for a naturalistic account of the creative, healing presence known in religious life as the divine Wieman struggled with many formulations. Over a period of half a century his understanding expanded, his self-criticism led him to revisions, his interest and focus shifted. He spoke at different times of the principle of concretion, progressive integration, the growth of good, creative synthesis, creativity, the creative event, and creative interchange. He was moved by a sense of our culture's urgent need for a concrete understanding of that process which saves and fulfills, and seems to have had a growing sense that his work was not being received as he wished.[1]

One autumn, as the faculty of the Divinity School reassembled for the new academic year, the church historian Wilhelm Pauck approached Wieman, put his arm around his shoulder, and with the warmth and gusto for which he was known and loved, he said, "Well Henry, what are you calling it now?" Wieman laughed and later said that something loosened within him and he was freed from a feeling of discouragement.[2] Why is the saying of Pauck comic? And why was it liberating?

God's Fools

One of the earliest influences on Wieman was the evolutionary philosopher Henri Bergson, whose concept of the *elan vital* or "vital force" which drives the evolutionary process has a family resemblance to some of Wieman's formulations. Bergson is unusual among modern philosophers in that he also developed a theory of the comic; he said that the ludicrous has a quality of stiffness and artificiality which resists creative evolution because it takes its present state as final. This is what Wieman would call resistance to creative transformation. Bergson may have inspired Wieman to develop his own somewhat different account of the relation of laughter and creative transformation.

According to Wieman, what strikes us as funny is "the sense of incongruity when . . . incongruity is suddenly resolved into a higher synthesis" of intensified experience.[3] He gives the example of the infant's delight at the game of peek-a-boo; the parent's appearance and disappearance amount to an incongruity, but when they occur repeatedly in sequence they are united as parts of an intelligible whole, and in this whole the experience of each phase is made more vivid through its relation with the other. The result is release and joy.

Similarly, in a joke two or more meanings are connected in a way which seems incongruous and momentarily disconcerting; when we see the point, we perceive that the apparently incompatible factors fit together into a larger totality of meaning, and the discrepancy is then known as revealing the factors present in the whole by contrast. As an example, Wieman tells of a newcomer to America who struggled with a language in which "though," "bough," "tough," and "cough" are pronounced differently. He gave up in despair and booked passage back to his place of origin when he saw the headline "Campaign pronounced success!" I cannot resist presenting an example of my own. We have seen that Wieman misunderstood Dewey's use of the term "God;" one of my colleagues said this is quite understandable because "reading Dewey is like swimming in oatmeal." You see in these jokes that an initial conflict of meanings yields to an insight, and then it becomes a richer harmony because of the contrast; what began as a conflict ends in an experience of unification in which we see and understand more than we did.

But notice that this is an instance of that process which Wieman called creative synthesis. The comic

> is the experience of overcoming conflict by resolving it into a richer synthesis of mutually vivifying parts. It is the experience of growth or progressive integration.[4]

For Wieman, laughter reveals that we find delight in the experience of creative synthesis, the universal process in which diverse elements are transformed by being related into a whole in which the powers of the parts are intensified. Wieman finds it significant that something deep in our nature takes joy in the process in which conflict is overcome in an unexpected unification, in which the parts are mutually enhancing.

In . . . laughter we reveal that our nature is made for God if it truly be that God is this creative synthesis which we have called growth working throughout the world. If God works always to bring diverse and conflicting activities into relations of mutual support and mutual enhancement with unpredictable emergents, then we see in our laughter that there is something in us deeper than conscious intent which rises up in joy when this quality in the work of God suddenly appears before us in swift and easily comprehended form.[5]

Our capacity for laughter shows that we are created and sustained by creative synthesis and our lives are fulfilled when we participate in its working.

The theory is extended in the observation that, for the delight of laughter to occur, we must bring both the conflict and its resolution into a richer synthesis without fear or a sense of threat. If the child is frightened by the sudden appearance of a face it will not laugh; if you feel that your identification with the revered philosopher Dewey is threatened by the ridicule implied in my joke about swimming in oatmeal, then you will not experience the comic. For an experience to be comical, you must be able to perceive it without regard for personal loss or gain; if, instead, you are intent on your own advantage or disadvantage, then at least on this occasion you have no sense of humor. But then this means that to laugh is to transcend self-concern for at least a moment. Once again, we see that the requirement for the working of progressive integration is non-attachment to the present order of our lives.

To lack a sense of humor is to be so absorbed in personal interests that we cannot let go and take delight in creative synthesis. (And from the point of view of Bergson's idea of the comic, such a person becomes ridiculous.) In humor we yield up concern for our own needs and goals and take delight in that larger process in which supportive connections are woven. To lack a sense of humor is to be self-absorbed, to cling to the present order of our lives; to laugh is to let go of this clinging and to be momentarily freed from self-concern.

Wieman concludes that this analysis illustrates a truth of religious faith: fulfillment in life comes from self-forgetfulness, from giving ourselves over to the operation of creative synthesis as "fools for God." The medieval idea of the carefree saint as God's fool unites the saintly and the comic, and Wieman explains that in laughter we experience for a moment a tendency which, when fully developed, is that self-forgetful devotion to growth seen in the highest form of religious living. He says, "laughter shows that we are made by nature to find our greatest joy in serving and delighting in the unlimited growth of organic connection."[6] Laughter allows us to take lightly our own programs and to see our achievements as trivial, compared to the richness which may come to be through the unforeseen working of creative synthesis. This is the religious meaning of the comical.

When we understand that an action or a saying is meant to be funny, we easily set aside concern for our own advantage or disadvantage. When greater issues are involved, and the unpredictable working of progressive integration is more profound, then we no longer have the comic. Perhaps the sacrifice of existing goods for the sake of emerging good involves tragic loss, but this too may be accompanied by a kind of resolution. For Wieman the basic principle is the same; it is "joy in the creative synthesis of interests previously diverse and conflicting, the synthesis occurring in disregard of the self-centered interests of individual or group."[7]

The jovial Pauck placed in contrast Wieman's earnest and single-minded quest for understanding and the image of a man who has only one idea but many names for it. This provided a comic way of looking at a serious task and its discouragements, and Wieman laughed and felt release.

The Theistic Stance without the Supernatural God

If we ask about Wieman's contribution to religious thought, we might recur to the phrase used in the first chapter: his naturalistic theism makes possible the theistic stance without the supernatural God. The elements central to this stance are openness to gifts and the yielding of the present order of our lives, so that transformation may occur. I believe Wieman intends only to address those for whom classical theism is problematic. He provides them with a way of seeing that inculcates a personal stance toward life which is open to the hidden supportiveness of those processes in nature, in our relationships, in our bodies, and in our minds, all of which work for growth and wholeness beyond our capacity to know or control. He identifies the structure of creativity at work on all levels of existence in such a way that commitment may be given to this creativity rather than to the results of its working in the past, so that we may be willing to yield up the present order of our lives for the sake of further growth.

Paradoxically, the liberal is the true conservative, in that the naturalistic reconstruction of the concept of God makes possible the preservation of the values essential to theistic faith in a changed cultural situation. This interpretation of Wieman is based on the conviction that he is primarily a theologian and not a religious philosopher. I take theology to be the attempt to give a rational account of the faith of a believing community, whereas religious philosophy is a disinterested quest for a truth we will be able to believe but do not yet possess. Wieman sought to make available to his time that kind of faith that transcends loss, suffering, and death because it is detached from created goods and centers on the creative source of good. His inquiry was simply for a concept of nature's grace that would make this theistic faith available to skeptical minds. So he said again and again, if it is not the supernatural, personal God which is the source of human good, then some recurrent event in nature must be. Wieman's student Bernhardt is by contrast a philosopher, one who seeks through reason for a plausible belief, and not a theologian using reason to express an old faith in a new way; his investigations thus lead him to reject traditional theistic values and to substitute for them a form of stoicism.

If we view Wieman's work in this way, criticism of his thought should begin with the question, is creativity an adequate expression of at least a liberal version of theistic faith? Wieman rejected the subjectivism of nineteenth century Protestant liberalism and sought to revive the sense of the reality of the divine; yet his theological realism was itself a reconstruction of traditional ideas—in short, a form of liberalism. Is creativity adequate as a conceptual basis for theistic faith?

I have said that the concept of the event of creative interchange is defective, arguing that disinterest in the cosmic dimension of creativity weakens Wieman's account of the religious life of Jesus. Even if the transformative power at work in the circle which centered on him is creative interchange, that openness to transformation of the self, which is its chief requirement, was based in the religion of Jesus on trust in a gracious creativity which is cosmic in scope. Further, Wieman's claim that creative interchange is the sole source of the transformation of the self and the widening of its appreciable world is not so much a discovery as a verbal flourish, since he includes this kind of growth in the very definition of creative interchange. We are left with the commonplace that sometimes communication is transformative (and then we may say the creative event in all its phases is present) and sometimes it is not. His response to this objection was to call for further research.

In fact, social and personal life depend on a larger non-human matrix which in turn, depends on the working of creative synthesis. New meanings and an enriched perception come about through the mysterious working of creative synthesis in human relationships and in the mind itself, and this creativity sometimes manifest in communication is simply one instance of a larger tendency.

What, then, are we to make of Wieman's evident discontent with the lack of specificity in the idea of creative synthesis and his increasing interest in creativity in communication? Wieman's work of the 'thirties leaves us with a concept, creative synthesis, which is valuable primarily for its power to inculcate in us the theistic stance without belief in a supernatural God. The history of Protestantism shows that a religion of trust in the mystery of grace is at first liberating but in the long run hard to bear; the mystery of grace calls for trust, and we would rather have things under our control. So in Calvin's Geneva and elsewhere, the religion of free grace led in time to a life of obedience and works as proofs that grace was present and sure. The manifest replaced the mysterious. This pattern is evident in Wieman: *trust* in that creativity which works where, when, and how it will is replaced with the *work* of creating conditions in communication in which creativity is bound to become manifest.

People who prefer the humanistic or pantheistic forms of naturalistic religious philosophy refer to what I am calling Wieman's theistic stance as his residual Calvinism. Here, I am claiming that he also retains some of the contradictions and internal tensions of that Reformation faith.

No, Wieman is at his best as he elaborates his concept of progressive integration as a recurrent, structured event manifest on all levels of existence. Here he goes beyond the conceptual theism of his colleagues Ames and Mathews, to identify the pattern of creativity, the building of relationships which enhance and magnify the powers of the elements ingredient in the process. If we ask for a more specific concept, if we demand to know what causes this recurrent event, we fail to understand Wieman's pragmatist understanding of ideas. Our concepts are tools in the adjustment of organism and environment, and not manifestations of a superhuman and adaptively superfluous Platonic power to grasp the ultimate nature of reality. If creative synthesis disappoints, and what we want is the discovery of a hidden power or being behind it, we have not yet understood the instrumentalist nature of ideas. They function to put us into relation with events, without disclosing their metaphysical reality. To pragmatists, events are all that is available, so it will not do to contrast ideas as guides to experience with another sort of understanding. The latter is simply not available.

Wieman is thus not like those naturalistic philosophers who feel an urge to reinvent religion and claim that now that we know that nature is all there is, we must become humanists or pantheists. Rather, Wieman accepts the nature of religious life as given, and seeks only to reconceive the divine in naturalistic terms. The elements in this givenness are the sense that human good depends on a power that works beyond human knowledge and effort, readiness for personal change, and non-attachment to existing good.

Notes

Introduction

1 Henry Nelson Wieman, "Intellectual Autobiography," in Robert Bretall, ed., *The Empirical Theology of Henry Nelson Wieman* (New York, Macmillan, 1963), p. 6.

2 Henry Nelson Wieman, "The Confessions of a Religious Seeker," *American Journal of Theology and Philosophy*, vol. 12 (May & September 1991), p. 72. This posthumously published essay was a longer version of the "Intellectual Autobiography" which appeared in Bretall, op. cit.. The editors of the journal state that the original was written in the 'forties. This seems likely because the essay refers to a forthcoming book which was to be called *The Problem of Civilizations*, which I take to be *The Directive in History*, published in 1949. The essay also refers to Wieman's retirement, which occurred in 1947, as recent.

3 Wieman, "Intellectual Autobiography," *loc. cit.*

4 *Ibid.*, p. 3.

5 Henry Nelson Wieman, "How Do We Know God?" *Journal of Religion*, vol. XXI (October 29, 1924), pp. 561–572.

6 Henry Nelson Wieman, "The Problem of Mysticism," in Alfred P. Stiernotte, ed., *Mysticism and the Modern Mind* (New York, Liberal Arts Press, 1959), pp. 23, 25.

7 Henry Nelson Wieman, *Religious Experience and Scientific Method* (New York, Macmillan, 1926), pp. 225–228.

8 Wieman, "The Problem of Mysticism," p. 25.

Chapter One

1 For Santayana's critique of pantheism see *Reason in Religion* (New York, Scribners, 1905), pp. 127–177.

2 See Bernard Loomer, "The Size of God," in William Dean and Larry E. Axel, eds., *The Size of God: the Theology of Bernard Loomer in Context* (Macon, Ga., Mercer University Press, 1987); Marvin C. Shaw, "The Romantic Love of Evil: Loomer's Proposal of a Reorientation in Religious Naturalism," *American Journal of Theology and Philosophy*, vol. 10 (January 1989), pp. 33–42.

3 See Bernard Meland, "The Root and Form of Wieman's Thought," in Robert Bretall, ed., *The Empirical Theology of Henry Nelson Wieman* (New York, Macmillan, 1963), pp. 50–53.

4 A.E. Haydon, *The Quest of the Ages* (New York, Harpers, 1929). E.S. Ames, "The Validity of the Idea of God," *Journal of Religion*, vol. I (September 1921), pp. 462–481.

5 Edward Scribner Ames, *Religion* (New York, Henry Holt, 1929), pp. 127–130.

6 *Ibid.*, pp. 131–132, 149–151, 170–171.

7 *Ibid.*, p. 151.

8 *Ibid.*, p. 32.

9 *Ibid.*, p. 173.

10 *Ibid.*, pp. 132–133.

11 *Ibid.*, p. 134.

12 *Ibid.*, pp. 173–174.

13 *Ibid.*, pp. 133–134, 173–175.

14 *Ibid.*, p. 154.

15 *Ibid.*, p. 178.

16 *Ibid.*, p. 154.

17 *Ibid.*, p. 158.

18 *Ibid.*, pp. 146–148, 151–158.

19 *Ibid.*, pp. 178–179.

20 *Ibid.*, p. 44–45.

21 Shailer Mathews, *The Growth of the Idea of God* (New York, Macmillan, 1931), p. 207.

22 Shailer Mathews, *The Atonement and the Social Process* (New York, Macmillan, 1930), p. 185.

23 Mathews, *The Growth of the Idea of God*, p. 217.

24 *Ibid.*, p. 216.

25 *Ibid.*, p. 214.

26 Shailer Mathews, *Is God Emeritus?* (New York, Macmillan, 1940), pp. 27–29.

27 Mathews, *The Growth of the Idea of God*, p. 6.

28 *Ibid.*

29 Mathews, *The Atonement and the Social Process*, pp. 185–187.

30 Mathews, *The Growth of the Idea of God*, p. 215.

31 *Ibid.*, p. 226.

32 *Ibid.*, p. 220.

33 Mathews, *Is God Emeritus?*, p. 38.

34 *Ibid.*, p. 34.

35 Mathews, *The Growth of the Idea of God*, p. 234.

36 Mathews, *Is God Emeritus?*, pp. 10–11.

37 *Ibid.*, p. 35.

38 Mathews, *The Growth of the Idea of God*, p. 219.

39 *Ibid.*, p. 221.

40 Mathews, *Is God Emeritus?*, p. 29.

41 *Ibid.*, pp. 29–31.

42 *Ibid.*, pp. 40–42, 58–59; cf. *The Growth of the Idea of God*, pp. 226, 232–234.

43 Mathews, *The Growth of the Idea of God*, p. 194.

44 *Ibid.*, pp. 193-195.

45 *Ibid.*, pp. 227-228.

46 Bernard Meland contrasts the "conceptual theism" of Ames and Mathews with Wieman's view of the divine as a "structured event" in *op. cit.*, pp. 52–53.

Chapter Two

1 Henry Nelson Wieman and Walter Marshall Horton, *The Growth of Religion* (Chicago, Willett, Clark, 1938) p. 345. All quotations from this book are from the chapters written by Wieman.

2 Henry Nelson Wieman and Regina Westcott-Wieman, *Normative Psychology of Religion* (New York, Thomas Y. Crowell, 1935) p. 185. All quotations from this book are from the chapters written by H.N. Wieman. Henry Nelson Wieman, *Methods of Private Religious Living* (New York, Macmillan, 1929), pp. 52–53.

3 *Methods*, p. 47.

4 *Ibid.*, p. 59.

5 *Normative Psychology of Religion*, p. 46.

6 *Ibid.*, p. 137.

7   *The Growth of Religion*, p. 338.

8   *Ibid.*, pp. 348–349.

9   *Ibid.*, p. 267.

10 *Ibid.*, p. 351.

11 *Ibid.*, p. 434.

12 *Methods of Private Religious Living*, p. 56.

13 *The Growth of Religion*, p. 315.

14 *Ibid.*, p. 353.

15 *Ibid.*, pp. 362–363. During this period, Wieman went so far as to justify the use of the term "Father" for God to portray our dependence upon creative synthesis, although he also refers to that which sustains us as a "mothering matrix." He used the pronoun "he" to refer to God because he felt "it" sounded negative and impersonal, although he did use the impersonal form occasionally, as in the quotation from *Methods of Private Religious Living*, p. 59 above.

16 *Methods of Private Religious Living*, p. 58.

17 *The Growth of Religion*, pp. 265–266.

18 *Normative Psychology of Religion*, p. 164.

19 *Ibid.*

20 *The Growth of Religion*, p. 33.

21 *Ibid.*, p. 377.

22 *Methods of Private Religious Living*, pp. 23–24.

23 *Ibid.*, p. 27.

24 Martin Heidegger, *Discourse on Thinking* (New York, Harper & Row, 1966) p. 68.

25 Viktor Frankl; *Man's Search for Meaning: an Introduction to Logotherapy*, rev. ed. (New York, Washington Square, 1963) p. 194; *The Doctor and the Soul: from Psychotherapy to Logotherapy*, 2nd ed. (New York, Alfred A. Knopf, 1966) p. 221 ff. See also my *The Paradox of Intention* (Atlanta, Scholars Press, 1988); and "Paradoxical Intention in the Life and Thought of William James," *American Journal of Theology and Philosophy*, vol. 7 (January 1986), pp. 5–16.

26 *Methods of Private Religious Living*, p. 194.

27 *The Growth of Religion*, pp. 307–311, 464; *Methods of Private Religious Living*, p. 147, and ch. VII; the concept is more fully developed and centers more clearly on the expansion of the mind through the communication of perspectives in *The Growth of Religion*.

28 *The Growth of Religion*, p. 369.

29 *Ibid.*, p. 384.

30 For Wieman's theological realism and the link with Karl Barth and others, see Henry Nelson Wieman, "God and Value" in Douglas C. Macintosh, ed., *Religious Realism* (New York, Macmillan, 1931). Wieman's "residual Calvinism" is mentioned in Daniel Day Williams, "Wieman as a Christian Theologian," in Robert W. Bretall, *The Empirical Theology of Henry Nelson Wieman* (New York, Macmillan Company, 1963), p. 78.

31 *Methods of Private Religious Living*, p. 35.

Chapter Three

1 Henry Nelson Wieman, *Religious Experience and Scientific* Method (New York, Macmillan, 1926), p. 9.

2 Henry Nelson Wieman, *The Wrestle of Religion with Truth* (New York, Macmillan, 1927), pp. 158–160.

3 *Ibid.*, p. 22.

4 *Religious Experience and Scientific Method*, p. 15. Interest in religious experience as the unique datum of religious thought is typical of the period and is related to the influence of William James' *Varieties of Religious Experience* (New York, Longmans Green, 1902) and William Ernest Hocking's *The Meaning of God in Human Experience* (New Haven, Yale University Press, 1912).

5 *Ibid.*, p. 39. The concept of immediate experience as a "blooming, buzzing confusion" prior to its being organized by concepts and habits of response appears widely at this time, and reflects the influence of William James' *Principles of Psychology* (New York, Henry Holt, 1890), ch. 9. In developing this concept, Wieman specifically quotes Alfred North Whitehead's *Concept of Nature* (London, Cambridge University Press, 1920): "The immediate fact for awareness is the whole occurrence of nature;" Wieman, op. cit, p. 176.

6 John Dewey, *Experience and Nature*, 1st edition (Chicago, Open Court, 1925), ch. V; Alfred North Whitehead, *Science and the Modern World* (New York, Macmillan, 1925), ch. XI.

7 *The Wrestle of Religion with Truth*, p. 185.

8 *Ibid.*, p. 189.

9 Henry Nelson Wieman, *The Source of Human Good* (Chicago, University of Chicago, 1946), p. 34.

10 *Ibid.*, p. 18.

11 *Ibid.*, p. 56.

12 *Ibid.*, p. 58.

13 John Dewey, *Philosophy and Civilization* (New York, Minton Balch, 1931), p. 211.

14 For the distinction between the qualitative and instrumental aspects of events, see John Dewey, *Experience and Nature*, 2nd edition (New York, W.W. Norton, 1929), chs. III and IV; the concept of communication as the ground of meaning is in the same work, pp. 166–202, and in John Dewey, *Philosophy and Civilization*, pp. 187–211

15 *The Source of Human Good*, p. 76.

16 Wieman lists six functions performed by the God of supernatural belief and claims that the creative event fulfills all of them. (1) The creative event directs the commitment of faith away from all created good. (2) It establishes a vision of righteousness beyond that embodied in the standards of any given time or place. (3) It establishes a bond between people deeper than affection, race, institutional loyalty, or devotion to common ideals. (4) It portrays evil as more serious than the mere destruction of any created good. (5) It presents the moral obligation laid upon us which overrides any demand made by society, tradition, ideals, institutions, or persons. (6) It opens possibilities of transformation beyond the mere effect of human effort or moral striving. Wieman was concerned to point out this functional equivalence because he believed that as the older supernaturalism looses its power it becomes more important to show that some actual reality underlies the myth. *Ibid.*, pp. 264–265.

17 This often-expressed objection is seen in the title of one of Wieman's popular essays, "The Waste We Cannot Afford!" *Unitarian-Universalist Register-Leader*, vol. 143 (November, 1962).

18 *The Source of Human Good*, chs. VII, VIII, and "Technical Postscript;" Henry Nelson Wieman, *Man's Ultimate Commitment* (Carbondale, Ill., Southern Illinois University, 1958), ch. IV.

Chapter Four

1 John Herman Randall, Jr., "George Santayana: Naturalizing the Imagination," *Journal of Philosophy*, vol. 51 (January 21, 1954), pp. 50–52.

2 George Santayana, *Reason in Religion* (New York, Scribners, 1905), p. 212.

3 John Herman Randall, Jr., "The Latent Idealism of a Materialist: a Review of Santayana's Realm of Matter," *Journal of Philosophy*, vol. 28 (November 19, 1931), pp. 647–648.

4 Eliseo Vivas, "From *The Life of Reason* to *The Last Puritan*," in Paul A. Schilpp, ed., *The Philosophy of George Santayana* (Evanston, Northwestern University Press), p. 350.

5 George Santayana, "Dewey's Naturalistic Metaphysics," *Journal of Philosophy*, vol. 22 (December 3, 1925), p. 680.

6 John Dewey, "Half-Hearted Naturalism," *Journal of Philosophy*, vol. 24 (February 3, 1927), p. 63.

7 Henry Nelson Wieman, "Religion in John Dewey's Philosophy," *Journal of Religion*, vol. 11 (January 1931), pp. 1–19.

8 John Dewey, *A Common Faith* (New Haven, Yale University, 1934), p. 33.

9 *Ibid.*, p. 42.

10 *Ibid.*, p. 50–51.

11 *Ibid.*, p. 52.

12 *Ibid.*, p. 51.

13 *Ibid.*, p. 25. Elsewhere Dewey refers to the sense of dependence in the theology of Friedrich Schleiermacher as the heart of the religious attitude. John Dewey, *The Quest for Certainty: a Study of the Relation of Knowledge and Action* (New York, Minton Balch, 1929), p. 307. Again, he writes that "goods are by grace not of ourselves." John Dewey, *Experience and Nature* 2nd ed. (New York, W.W. Norton, 1929), p. 43. "The fact that civilization endures and culture continues—and sometimes advances—is evidence e that human hopes and purposes find a basis and support in nature. As the developing growth of an individual from embryo to maturity is the result of interaction of organism with surroundings, so culture is the product not of human efforts . . . put forth in a void or just upon themselves, but of prolonged and cumulative interaction with environment." John Dewey, *Art as Experience* (New York, Minton Balch, 1934), p. 28.

14 *Ibid.*, pp. 53–54.

15 Henry Nelson Wieman, "John Dewey's *Common Faith*," *Christian Century*, vol. 51 (November 14, 1934), pp.1450–1452.

16 E.E. Aubrey, "Is John Dewey a Theist?" *Christian Century*, vol. 51 (December 5, 1934), pp. 1550.

17 Henry Nelson Wieman, "Is John Dewey a Theist?" *Christian Century*, vol. 51 (December 5, 1934), pp. 1550–1551.

18 John Dewey, "Is John Dewey a Theist?" *Christian Century*, vol. 51 (December 5, 1934), pp. 1551–1552.

19 Wieman, *Ibid.*, p. 1552.

20 John Dewey, "A God or *the* God: a Review of *Is There a God? a Conversation* by D.C. MacIntosh, M. Otto, and H.N. Wieman," *Christian Century*, vol. 50 (February 8, 1933), pp. 193–196.

21 *The Humanist*, vol. 13 (March-April 1953), pp. 58–61.

22 Wieman, *Ibid.*, p. 1553.

23 Charles Clayton Morrison, "The Philosophers and God," *Christian Century*, vol. 51 (December 12, 1934), pp. 1582-1584. Charles Hartshorne, "Three Questions for Professor Dewey," *Christian Century*, vol. 52 (January 9, 1935), pp. 51–53.

24 Charles Hartshorne, *Beyond Humanism: Essays in the New Philosophy of Nature* (Chicago, Willett Clark, 1937), p. 56.

25 Years later Wieman wrote some humorous lines on the problem of interpreting Dewey; he may have been thinking of this debate. "I never quite understand what he is saying, but I am generally enthusiastic about it. . . . His ideas are sufficiently inchoate so that I can almost always make out of them something a little different from what he intended, and nearer to what I think he ought to say." "Confessions of a Religious Seeker," *American Journal of Theology and Philosophy*, vol. 12 (May & September 1991), p. 102. This is a posthumous publication of an essay written in about 1947.

Chapter Five

1 An earlier study of the Wieman-Bernhardt discussion is deficient, I believe, in that it did not see the central issue as the choice between pantheism and naturalistic theism. See J. Alton Templin, "A God of Power or a God of Value: Another Look at the Debates between William Bernhardt and Henry Nelson Wieman, 1942–1943," in W. Creighton Peden and Larry E. Axel, *God, Values, and Empiricism: Issues in Philosophical Theology* (Macon, Ga., Mercer University Press, 1989), pp. 220–230.

2 William H. Bernhardt, "An Analytical Approach to the God-Concept," *Religion in the Making*, vol. 2 (March 1942), pp. 252–263.

3 Henry Nelson Wieman, "Can God be Perceived?" *Journal of Religion*, vol. 23 (January 1943), pp. 23–32.

4 William H. Bernhardt, "The Cognitive Quest for God," *Journal of Religion*, vol. 23 (April 1943), pp. 91–102; "God as Dynamic Determinant," *Journal of Religion*, vol. 23 (October 1943), pp. 276–285.

5 Bernhardt later developed a complete statement of this theory of religion: William H. Bernhardt, *A Functional Philosophy of Religion* (Denver, Criterion Press, 1958). See also William C. Tremmel, *Religion: What Is It?* (New York, Holt, Rinehart and Winston, 1976).

6 Bernhardt, "God as Dynamic Determinant," p. 281.

7 *Ibid.*, p. 283.

8 *Ibid.*, p. 284.

9 William H. Bernhardt, "Operational Theism," *Iliff Review*, vol. 16 (Winter 1959) pp. 21–33.

10 Bernhardt, "God as Dynamic Determinant," p. 285.

11 *Ibid.*

12 Henry Nelson Wieman, "Power and Goodness of God," *Journal of Religion*, vol. 23 (October 1943), pp. 266–275.

13 *Ibid.*, p. 266.

14 *Ibid.*, p. 267.

15 Wieman, "Can God be Perceived?," *Journal of Religion*, vol. 23 (January 1943), p. 27.

16 Wieman, "Power and Goodness of God," *Journal of Religion*, vol. 23 (October 1943), p. 275.

17 Bernhardt, "God as Dynamic Determinant," pp. 276–280.

18 Daniel Day Williams, "Wieman as a Christian Theologian," in Robert W. Bretall, *The Empirical Theology of Henry Nelson Wieman* (New York, Macmillan Company, 1963), pp. 73–74.

19 Henry Nelson Wieman, "Reply to Dubs and Bernhardt," *Journal of Religion*, vol. 24 (January 1944), pp. 56–58. The title under which the letter was printed includes reference to Homer H. Dubs, "Religious Naturalism: an Evaluation," *Journal of Religion*, vol. 23 (October 1943), pp. 258-256. This article includes a criticism of Wieman's naturalistic theism first encountered in chapter three, namely that the concept of creativity lacks unity; instances of creativity's action are numerically diverse and only have in common their creative character. Dubs' point was that supernatural theism is more coherent because it attributes all creative transformation to the action of a single agent.

20 *Ibid.*, p. 58.

21 *Ibid.*

22 *Ibid.*

Chapter Six

1 Henry Nelson Wieman, *Normative Psychology of Religion* (New York, Thomas Y. Crowell, 1935), p. 182.

2 *Ibid.*, pp. 170–171.

3 *Ibid.*, p. 185.

4 *Ibid.*, pp. 189–190.

5 Henry Nelson Wieman, *Man's Ultimate Commitment* (Carbondale, Ill., Southern Illinois University, 1958), p. 22.

6 *Ibid.*

7 *Ibid.*, pp. 33–34.

8 This conclusion was reached in discussion with Nancy Frankenberry. See Nancy Frankenberry, "Henry Nelson Wieman: Empirical Theism and Naturalism," in *Religion and Radical Empiricism* (Albany, State University of New York, 1987), pp. 113–129; Marvin C. Shaw, "Frankenberry's Critique and the Recovery of the Early Wieman," *American Journal of Theology and Philosophy*, vol. 13, May 1992, pp. 105–116; Nancy Frankenberry, "Reconstructing Religion without Revelation, Foundations, or Fideism: a Reply to My Critics," *American Journal of Theology and Philosophy*, vol. 13, May 1992, especially "Reply to Marvin Shaw," pp. 131–135.

Chapter Seven

1 Henry Nelson Wieman, *Intellectual Foundation of Faith* (New York, Philosophical Library, 1961), p. 1.

2 *Ibid.*, pp. 16–18.

3 Henry Nelson Wieman, *Man's Ultimate Commitment* (Carbondale, Southern Illinois University, 1958), p. 11.

4 Wieman, *Intellectual Foundation of Faith*, p. 4.

5 *Ibid.*, p. 6.

6 Wieman, *Man's Ultimate Commitment*, p. 11.

7 *Ibid.*, p. 23.

8 *Ibid.*, p. 149.

9 Wieman, *Intellectual Foundation of Faith*, p. 9.

10 Wieman, *Man's Ultimate Commitment*, p. 77.

11 I believe the idea that there can be unitarians of the first, second, and third persons was suggested by H. Richard Niebuhr, but the way the terms are defined here is my own. It also seems clear that some forms of Unitarian theology attempt to include all the functions and meanings mentioned, and simply reject the dogma of the three persons.

12 Bernard M. Loomer, "Wieman's Stature as a Contemporary Theologian," in Robert W. Bretall, ed., *The Empirical Theology of Henry Nelson Wieman* (New York, Macmillan, 1963), p. 393.

13 *Ibid.*

14 Wieman, *The Source of Human Good*, p. 39.

15 *Ibid.*, p. 40.

16 Wieman, *Intellectual Foundation of Faith*, p. 85.

17 *Ibid.*, p. 36.

18 Wieman, *The Source of Human Good*, p. 275.

19 *Ibid.*, p. 40. In *The Source of Human Good* this material is presented as an analysis of what occurred in the fellowship of Jesus, prior to Wieman's presentation of his own concept of the creative event. Nevertheless, Wieman's concept of creative interchange came first and is here being applied to the Christ-event in order to account for the personal transformation which occurred.

20 Henry Nelson Wieman, "What Is Most Important in Christianity?" in Cedric L. Hepler, ed., *Seeking a Faith for a New Age: Essays on the Interdependence of Religion, Science and Philosophy* (Metuchen, N.J., Scarecrow Press, 1975), p. 175; reprinted from *Religion in the Making*, vol. I, 1940–1941.

21 Wieman, *The Source of Human Good*, p. 44.

22 *Ibid.*, pp. 274–275. "What Is Most Important in Christianity?" in Hepler, *op. cit.*, pp. 174–175.

23 Wieman, "What Is Most Important in Christianity?" in Hepler, *op. cit.*, p. 175.

24 Wieman, *The Source of Human Good*, p. 41.

25 *Ibid.*, p. 269.

26 Henry Nelson Wieman, "Reply to Horton," in Bretall, *op. cit.*, p. 191.

27 Henry Nelson Wieman, "Reply to Weigel," in Bretall, *op. cit.*, p. 373.

28 Wieman, *Intellectual Foundation of Faith*, p. 35.

29 Wieman, *Man's Ultimate Commitment*, p. 271.

30 *Ibid.*, p. 272.

31 Wieman, "Reply to Weigel," in Bretall, *op. cit.*, p. 374.

32 Wieman, *Intellectual Foundation of Faith*, p. 55.

33 Henry Nelson Wieman, "Empiricism in Religious Philosophy," in Hepler, *op. cit.*, p. 153; reprinted from Leroy S. Rouner, *Philosophy, Religion, and the Coming World Civilization: Essays in Honor of William Ernest Hocking* (The Hague, Netherlands, Martinus Nijhof, 1966).

34 Wieman, *The Source of Human Good*, p. 269.

35 Henry Nelson Wieman, "Commitment for Theological Inquiry," in Hepler, *op. cit.*, p. 138; reprinted from *Journal of Religion*, vol. XLII (July 1962).

Conclusion

1 Henry Nelson Wieman, "The Confessions of a Religious Seeker," *American Journal of Theology and Philosophy*, vol. 12 (May and September 1991), p. 118.

2 The source of this story is Professor Edward Hobbs. Wilhelm Pauck related it at an annual dinner meeting of the New Testament Club of the Divinity School of the University of Chicago sometime in the late 'forties.

3 Henry Nelson Wieman, *The Growth of Religion* (Chicago, Willett, Clark, 1938), p. 459.

4 *Ibid.*

5 *Ibid.*, pp. 459–460.

6 *Ibid.*, p. 462.

7 *Ibid.*, p. 463.

Bibliography

Alexander, Samuel, *Space, Time, and Deity*, 2 vols. (London, Macmillan, 1927).

Ames, Edward Scribner, "The Validity of the Idea of God," *Journal of Religion*, vol. I (September 1921).

_____, *Religion* (New York, Henry Holt, 1929).

Aubrey, E.E., "Is John Dewey a Theist?" *Christian Century*, vol. 51 (December 5, 1934).

Bergson, Henri, *Creative Evolution* (New York, Henry Holt, 1911).

_____, *Laughter: an Essay on the Meaning of the Comic* (New York, Macmillan, 1928).

Bernhardt, William H., "An Analytical Approach to the God-Concept," *Religion in the Making*, vol. 2 (March 1942).

_____, "The Cognitive Quest for God," *Journal of Religion*, vol. 23 (April 1943).

_____, "God as Dynamic Determinant," *Journal of Religion*, vol. 23 (October 1943).

_____, *A Functional Philosophy of Religion* (Denver, Criterion Press, 1958).

_____, "Operational Theism," *Iliff Review*, vol. 16 (Winter 1959).

Bretall, Robert, ed., *The Empirical Theology of Henry Nelson Wieman* (New York, Macmillan, 1963).

Broyer, John A. and William Sherman Minor, *Creative Interchange* (Carbondale, Ill., Southern Illinois University, 1982).

Cobb, John B., Jr., *Living Options in Protestant Theology: a Survey of Methods* (Philadelphia, Westminster, 1962).

Dean, William, *American Religious Empiricism* (Albany, N.Y., State University of New York, 1986).

_____, and Larry E. Axel, eds., *The Size of God: the Theology of Bernard Loomer in Context* (Macon, Ga., Mercer University Press, 1987).

Dewey, John, *Experience and Nature*, (Chicago, Open Court, 1925), rev. ed. (New York, W.W. Norton, 1929).

_____, "Half-Hearted Naturalism," *Journal of Philosophy*, vol. 24 (February 3, 1927).

_____, *The Quest for Certainty: a Study of the Relation of Knowledge and Action* (New York, Minton Balch, 1929).

_____, *Philosophy and Civilization* (New York, Minton Balch, 1931).

_____, "A God or *the* God: a Review of Is There a God? a Conversation by D.C. MacIntosh, M. Otto, and H.N. Wieman," *Christian Century*, vol. 50 (February 8, 1933).

_____, *A Common Faith* (New Haven, Yale University, 1934).

_____, *Art as Experience* (New York, Minton Balch, 1934).

_____, "Is John Dewey a Theist?" *Christian Century*, vol. 51 (December 5, 1934).

Dubs, Homer H., "Religious Naturalism: an Evaluation," *Journal of Religion*, vol. 23 (October 1943).

Frankenberry, Nancy, *Religion and Radical Empiricism* (Albany, State University of New York, 1987).

_____, "Reconstructing Religion without Revelation, Foundations, or Fideism: a Reply to My Critics," *American Journal of Theology and Philosophy*, vol. 13, May 1992.

Frankl, Viktor, *Man's Search for Meaning: an Introduction to Logotherapy*, rev. ed. (New York, Washington Square,1963).

_____, *The Doctor and the Soul: from Psychotherapy to Logotherapy*, 2nd ed. (New York, Alfred A. Knopf, 1966).

Hartshorne, Charles, "Three Questions for Professor Dewey," *Christian Century*, vol. 52 (January 9, 1935).

_____, *Beyond Humanism: Essays in the New Philosophy of Nature* (Chicago, Willett Clark, 1937).

Haydon, A. Eustace, *The Quest of the Ages* (New York, Harpers, 1929).

Heidegger, Martin, *Discourse on Thinking* (New York, Harper & Row, 1966).

Hepler, Cedric L., ed., *Seeking a Faith for a New Age: Essays on the Interdependence of Religion, Science and Philosophy* (Metuchen, N.J., Scarecrow Press, 1975).

Hocking, William Ernest, *The Meaning of God in Human Experience: a Philosophical Study of Religion* (New Haven, Yale University Press, 1912).

James, William, *Principles of Psychology*, 3 vols. (New York, Henry Holt, 1890).

_____, *Varieties of Religious Experience* (New York, Longmans Green, 1902).

Kurtz, Paul, ed., *Humanist Manifestos I and II* (Buffalo, N.Y., Prometheus Books, 1973).

Loomer, Bernard M., "Wieman's Stature as a Contemporary Theologian," in Robert W. Bretall, ed., *The Empirical Theology of Henry Nelson Wieman* (New York, Macmillan, 1963).

_____, "The Size of God" in William Dean and Larry E. Axel, eds., *The Size of God: the Theology of Bernard Loomer in Context* (Macon, Ga., Mercer University Press, 1987).

MacIntosh, Douglas C., ed., *Religious Realism* (New York, Macmillan, 1931).

Martin, James A., *Empirical Philosophies of Religion, with Special Reference to Boodin, Brightman, Hocking, Macintosh, and Wieman* (New York, King's Crown, 1945).

Mathews, Shailer, *The Faith of Modernism* (New York, Macmillan, 1924).

_____, *The Atonement and the Social Process* (New York, Macmillan, 1930).

_____, *The Growth of the Idea of God* (New York, Macmillan, 1931).

_____, *Is God Emeritus?* (New York, Macmillan, 1940).

Meland, Bernard, "The Root and Form of Wieman's Thought" in Robert Bretall, ed., *The Empirical Theology of Henry Nelson Wieman* (New York, Macmillan, 1963).

Minor, William Sherman, ed., *Charles Hartshorne and Henry Nelson Wieman* (Carbondale, Ill, Foundation for Creative Philosophy, 1969).

_____, *Creativity in Henry Nelson Wieman* (Metuchen, N.J., Scarecrow Press, 1977).

Morgan, C. Lloyd, *Emergent Evolution* (London, Williams & Norgate, 1923).

Morrison, Charles Clayton, "The Philosophers and God," *Christian Century*, vol. 51 (December 12, 1934).

Peden, W. Creighton, *Wieman's Empirical Process Philosophy* (Washington, D.C., University Press of America, 1977).

_____, and Larry E. Axel, *God, Values, and Empiricism: Issues in Philosophical Theology* (Macon, Ga., Mercer University Press, 1989).

Randall, John Herman, Jr., "The Latent Idealism of a Materialist: a Review of Santayana's *Realm of Matter*," *Journal of Philosophy*, vol. 28 (November 19, 1931).

_____, "George Santayana: Naturalizing the Imagination," *Journal of Philosophy*, vol. 51 (January 21, 1954).

Santayana, George, *Reason in Religion* (New York, Scribners, 1905).

_____, "Dewey's Naturalistic Metaphysics," *Journal of Philosophy*, vol. 22 (December 3, 1925).

Schilpp, Paul A., ed., *The Philosophy of George Santayana* (Evanston, Ill., Northwestern University).

Shaw, Marvin C., "Paradoxical Intention in the Life and Thought of William James," *American Journal of Theology and Philosophy*, vol. 7 (January 1986).

_____, *The Paradox of Intention* (Atlanta, Scholars Press, 1988).

_____, "The Romantic Love of Evil: Loomer's Proposal of a Reorientation in Religious Naturalism," *American Journal of Theology and Philosophy*, vol. 10 (January 1989).

_____, "Frankenberry's Critique and the Recovery of the Early Wieman,"*American Journal of Theology and Philosophy*, vol. 13 (May 1992).

Shea, William M., *The Naturalists and the Supernatural: Studies in Horizon and an American Philosophy of Religion* (Macon, Ga., Mercer University Press, 1984).

Smuts, Jan C., *Holism and Evolution* (London, Macmillan, 1926).

Stiernotte, Alfred P., ed., *Mysticism and the Modern Mind* (New York, Liberal Arts Press, 1959).

Stone, Jerome A. *The Minimalist Vision of Transcendence: a Naturalist Philosophy of Religion* (Albany, N.Y., State University of New York, 1992).

Templin, J. Alton, "A God of Power or a God of Value: Another Look at the Debates between William Bernhardt and Henry Nelson Wieman, 1942–1943," in W. Creighton Peden and Larry E. Axel, *God, Values, and Empiricism: Issues in Philosophical Theology* (Macon, Ga., Mercer University Press, 1989).

Tremmel, William C., *Religion: What Is It?* (New York, Holt, Rinehart and Winston, 1976).

Vivas, Eliseo, "From *The Life of Reason* to *The Last Puritan*," in Paul A. Schilpp, ed., *The Philosophy of George Santayana* (Evanston, Ill., Northwestern University).

Whitehead, Alfred North, *The Concept of Nature* (London, Cambridge University, 1920).

_____, *Science and the Modern World* (New York, Macmillan, 1925).

_____, *Religion in the Making* (New York, Macmillan, 1926).

_____, *Process and Reality* (New York, Macmillan, 1929).

Wieman, Henry Nelson, *The Organization of Interests: a Thesis Presented to the Department of Philosophy of Harvard University for the Degree Doctor of Philosophy, 1917*, ed. by Cedric L. Hepler (Washington, D.C., University Press of America, 1985).

_____, "How Do We Know God?" *Journal of Religion*, vol. 21 (October 29, 1924).

_____, *Religious Experience and Scientific Method* (New York, Macmillan, 1926).

_____, *The Wrestle of Religion with Truth* (New York, Macmillan, 1927).

_____, *Methods of Private Religious Living* (New York, Macmillan, 1929).

_____, "Religion in John Dewey's Philosophy," *Journal of Religion*, vol. 11 (January 1931).

_____, "God and Value" in Douglas C Macintosh, ed., *Religious Realism* (New York, Macmillan, 1931).

_____, "John Dewey's *Common Faith*," *Christian Century*, vol. 51 (November 14, 1934).

_____, "Is John Dewey a Theist?" *Christian Century*, vol. 51 (December 5, 1934).

_____, and Regina Westcott-Wieman, *Normative Psychology of Religion* (New York, Thomas Y. Crowell, 1935).

_____, and Walter Marshall Horton, *The Growth of Religion* (Chicago, Willett, Clark, 1938).

_____, "What Is Most Important in Christianity?" in Cedric L. Hepler, ed., *Seeking a Faith for a New Age: Essays on the Interdependence of Religion, Science and Philosophy* (Metuchen, N.J., Scarecrow Press, 1975); reprinted from the journal *Religion in the Making*, vol. I, 1940-1941.

_____, "Can God be Perceived?," *Journal of Religion*, vol. 23 (January 1943).

_____, "Power and Goodness of God," *Journal of Religion*, vol. 23 (October 1943).

_____, "Reply to Dubs and Bernhardt," *Journal of Religion*, vol. 24 (January 1944).

_____, *The Source of Human Good* (Chicago, University of Chicago, 1946).

_____, "The Confessions of a Religious Seeker," *American Journal of Theology and Philosophy*, vol. 12 (May and September 1991); written about 1947.

_____, *The Directive in History* (Boston, Beacon, 1949).

_____, *Man's Ultimate Commitment* (Carbondale, Ill., Southern Illinois University, 1958).

_____, "The Problem of Mysticism" in Alfred P. Stiernotte, ed., *Mysticism and the Modern Mind* (New York, Liberal Arts Press, 1959).

_____, *Intellectual Foundation of Faith* (New York, Philosophical Library, 1961).

_____, "Commitment for Theological Inquiry," in Cedric L. Hepler, ed., *Seeking a Faith for a New Age: Essays on the Interdependence of Religion, Science and Philosophy* (Metuchen, N.J., Scarecrow Press, 1975); reprinted from *Journal of Religion*, vol. 42 (July 1962).

_____, "The Waste We Cannot Afford!" *Unitarian-Universalist Register-Leader*, vol. 143 (November, 1962).

_____, "Intellectual Autobiography," in Robert Bretall, ed., *The Empirical Theology of Henry Nelson Wieman* (New York, Macmillan, 1963).

_____, "Empiricism in Religious Philosophy," in Cedric L. Hepler, ed., *Seeking a Faith for a New Age: Essays on the Interdependence of Religion, Science and Philosophy* (Metuchen, N.J., Scarecrow Press, 1975); reprinted from Leroy S. Rouner, ed., *Philosophy,*

Religion, and the Coming World Civilization: Essays in Honor of William Ernest Hocking (The Hague, Netherlands, Martinus Nijhof, 1966).

_____, *Religious Inquiry: Some Explorations* (Boston, Beacon, 1968).

Williams, Daniel Day, "Wieman as a Christian Theologian," in Robert W. Bretall, *The Empirical Theology of Henry Nelson Wieman* (New York, Macmillan Company, 1963).